The Bryant Library Sundial

The Bryant Library &
The Friends of Bryant Library
Gratefully Acknowledge This Gift
Donated in Memory of

Helene Fisher

~ Beloved Teacher ~
An inspiration to all who passed her way

REMEMBER *for* LIFE

Holocaust Survivors' Stories
of Faith and Hope

EDITED BY
Brad Hirschfield

2007 • 5768
The Jewish Publication Society
Philadelphia

JPS is a nonprofit educational association and the oldest and foremost publisher of Judaica in English in North America. The mission of JPS is to enhance Jewish culture by promoting the dissemination of religious and secular works, in the United States and abroad, to all individuals and institutions interested in past and contemporary Jewish life

Remember for Life
Edited by Brad Hirschfield

Copyright © 2006 by CLAL - The National Jewish Center for Learning and Leadership

2007 edition published by The Jewish Publication Society

.

No part of this book may be reproduced or transmitted in any form or by any means, electronic or mechanical, including photocopy, recording, or any information storage or retrieval system, except for brief passages in connection with a critical review, without permission in writing from the publisher:

The Jewish Publication Society
2100 Arch Street, 2nd floor
Philadelphia, PA 19103
www.jewishpub.org

Manufactured in the United States of America

07 08 09 10   10 9 8 7 6 5 4 3 2 1

ISBN 13: 978-0-8276-0875-7

LEVITICUS

NUMBERS

DEUTERONOMY

HOLIDAYS

INTRODUCTION

I am a fourth-generation American Jew who cannot name a single relative who perished in the *Shoah*. That reality will be shared by more and more of us, especially as we become the first generation to live without any individuals who can share direct accounts of their personal experiences during, before, and immediately after the Holocaust. There are only two options in the face of this reality: to forget what happened, which would be obscene; or to remember in new ways that remain meaningful for a new generation. The latter is what it means to remember for life.

Memory is always about choice. We can choose to remember the past in ways that will stir our anger and evoke our rage. We can choose to remember in ways that stimulate sadness and provoke pain. And we can choose to remember in ways that challenge us to take from the past those memories and lessons that we need right now in order to be the people we most want to be, and to help create the kind of world in which we most want to live. We can remember for life.

Nowhere is that kind of choice-making more important than in connection with the *Shoah*. And never has it been more important than it is right now, because we are the first generation that will live without the presence of those who can tell us in their own words what they have seen with their own eyes. We are the first generation who will not be able to rely on the direct experience of the survivors to help us understand what happened in those dark years.

While our reliance on their presence as the guarantor of our memory has been beneficial in so many ways, it leaves us now with two profound challenges. First, to acknowledge that continuing to remember as we have for the last sixty years will become increasingly impossible, and second, to appreciate the potent opportunity we have in creating the next generation of Holocaust memory, one that will be cherished not only for its own sake, but, like the memory of every other past tragedy in our people's past, as a point of embarkation for the next chapter in our eternal story. This book was created to rise to these two challenges.

Remember for Life connects our most ancient teachings with the lives of those who saw those teachings tested probably more than any other. Now we have the opportunity to learn from them the lessons that have always been embedded within that tradition, lessons about life and living to the fullest in every sense of the word.

When Sherman Jacobson, initial supporter of this work, and CLAL Executive Vice Chairman Donna Rosenthal sat down in my office two years ago, I had no way of knowing that the book you now hold in your hands would be produced. In fact, I never imagined working on any kind of volume about the Holocaust at all. But in the end, this book is not only about the Holocaust. It is about the sacred opportunity to remember the past in ways that will help guarantee the future.

Remember For Life continues an ancient tradition that dates back to the Hebrew Bible—a tradition of remembering traumatic events, such as the Exodus from Egypt, in ways that enhanced the lives of those who went free and the lives of all those around them. It is about choosing life—even, or perhaps especially, as we make our choices about how to remember the deadliest of times.

When Sherman came to my office, he brought a single request. He wanted to see what could be done to make

Holocaust memory a more regular part of the synagogue service. In truth, I was not sure how to answer him. I was worried that if I told him what I really thought, he would be upset, and it was apparent from the first moments of our initial meeting that he was such an intelligent and passionate man that that was the last thing I wanted to do. He noticed my hesitation and, in his gently forceful way, pushed me to respond.

I explained that I thought one *Yom Hashoah* a year was enough—that the rabbis of two thousand years ago were brilliant in their forcing virtually all of the rest of Jewish tragedy memory into three weeks in the summer, leaving the other forty-eight weeks of the year to focus not on remembering Jewish death, but on celebrating Jewish life. A sixteen-to-one life to death ratio seemed about right to me, and I did not really believe we needed to change that ratio by including a *Yom Hashoah* moment in each week's Shabbat morning service.

So he asked me, what should we do? I told him that we should invite the words of survivors into our lives on a regular basis, but not primarily as teachers about hatred and death. Instead, we must find a way to invite their presence as teachers of life, ethics, decency, and love. I wanted to see if we could actually begin to remember more often without always remembering more horror. I hope that we, the first generation that will live without them, might begin to honor the survivors of the *Shoah* as more than symbols of past horror and death—that we could come to see them as *rebbes*, as masters of the value of life and as guides about how to live the life we are given more fully and more deeply.

To that end, we have assembled this collection of stories taken from the words of the survivors themselves, edited them as little as possible, and present them to you as commentaries on the weekly Torah readings and holidays that fill our year. Our Torah is called a *Torat Hayim*, a living teaching, a teaching for life. We honor that tradition by sharing with you these teachers of that Torah.

This book helps us to remain connected to our past by focusing on its ability to help us live more fully in the present and create a richer future for ourselves and our world. With their stories, each of the people in this book teaches us about life and how it can be lived more meaningfully, more ethically, and more joyfully. That has always been the purpose of our Torah, and there are no better people to remind us of that than the story tellers in this book. They know that ours is a Torah of life, an eternal story that is assured by our willingness to link our own life stories to it, and to learn from them both.

In finding a few moments each week to share one of their stories, both they and the Torah from which we read will come more alive. And just as importantly, so will we. Torah into life and life into Torah—the ancient rhythms will continue, memory will be created, and wisdom will be shared, for life.

Brad Hirschfield, *Editor*
President, CLAL

בראשית GENESIS

Creativity

A violin was given to a 25 year old young man who couldn't play a single note. He was shivering, and the violin song sounded like screeching. The SS mockingly said, You want me to give you food for this? And they started beating and kicking him, and the kapos kicked him to death.

While they were pulling him out of the room I tried to sneak back into the barrack, but a kapo grabbed me and forced me to the middle of the floor and gave me the violin and says, Play! When I first entered that room, I thought that I'm going to play if I have a chance a sonatino by Dvorak or a piece by Fritz Kreisler, but in that bloodied room, nothing came to my mind, absolutely nothing, and I said, Oh my God, how does the sonatino start? How does the Fritz Kreisler piece start? How does anything start? I was so scared.

From my side of the eye, I notice that a kapo picked up an iron pipe and was walking toward me. Every nerve in my body knew that I'm gonna die, that it's the end, and I started saying within me, Shema Yisroel Adonai Eloheinu. He was less than two steps from me when my left hand and right hand started to move in perfect harmony and this beautiful Blue Danube came out with joy—loud, clear, like if I would have been playing that forever. Forgive me for putting it this way—like Heifetz would have played it.

And this kapo is waiting and just looking at the SS— when should I hit him? The SS held up his hand and he started to beat the rhythm—oompapa, oompapa, oompapa, because I played the Blue Danube—it's in three-quarter time. So he was beating and then he said hold it. From that time on, right then and there, I could play anything that I

wanted.

Now I'm gonna tell you something that you're not going to believe. I had never played the Blue Danube in my life before. Never. So, how did I play so gloriously the violin? In that room where the SS killed already two persons, or told the kapo to kill them? How? What happened there? How could that happen? It's only God, it's only God—God's hands were on my violin. There's no other way—that's how strongly I believe in God—it's a miracle—it was a miracle.

SHONY B.
Romania

# בראשית NOAH

Survival

We dressed, and it was a very hot day for Amsterdam, a very hot day. We dressed with three sets of clothes, one on top of another, because we had our rucksack ready ever since it started. It was June 20, 1943.

We were sitting by the window; the truck of the Germans was in front of our house. At 8:30 I said to Dan, let's lay down on the bed. Whatever rest we get now, if they get us, we have to stand the whole night because you were moved like cattle then, there were no fancy trains. We fell asleep, and we woke up at 5:30 in the morning, and it was over. They had forgotten us. That we are here today is not because we were smarter than anybody else. We just had luck. That's all there is to it.

That day our stamp on the identification card that had protected us was obsolete, so we didn't go out of the house yet. Then the rumors came: they will keep 170 families in Amsterdam. We were picked, but the wrong address was on the new pass. We lived in Reitzstraat number 7 and they put on Retiefstraat number 7. Would you believe it saved our life?

On the evening before Rosh Hashoneh, on September 28, they went to collect all these other people that had been left behind. They had us on the list on Retiefstraat so they never came to the right street.

After the war when we came out of hiding, we went to that address in the Retiefstraat. It just so happened that non-Jewish people lived there, and we found out that indeed that they called for us at that address. That's how we were saved. Not because we were smarter than anybody else. You know?

REGINA G.
Netherlands

LEKH LEKHA

Journey

I was told that I would stay in a big house in England, and there were two daughters, and that I would go to school. From the age of 10, I always wanted to be a doctor. I had quite a lot of ill health as a small child, and I think deep down going to study medicine was a way of acquiring knowledge and being able to cope with that. I mean, this is with hindsight. But there's nothing else I wanted to do.

I remember leaving Prague on the old express train, the Schnellzug as we called it. I do remember the two German soldiers, the border people, looking at my passport. That is the only moment I remember of slight tension.

We went straight from Prague to Calais. There I went on the boat, and it was very rough; I remember being very seasick. The boat came to Dover. And that's where I was met by this family—Leon—it was Alderman and Mrs. H.A. Leon.

They were Jewish and they lived in Quay Road in Richmond Surrey. I remember it was quite a big house, and I shared a room with the younger daughter, and I remember waking up the first morning and saying, I slept "how a princess." I was teased about that for a long time. I said "how a princess" because my English wasn't very good. But that is how I slept.

CHARLOTTE B.
Czechoslovakia

בְּרֵאשִׁית VA-YERA'

Hospitality

While I was in the Lublin ghetto, I wrote my father a letter because he didn't know where I was. After waiting two, three weeks without getting an answer, I choose to go back to Krakow.

I was walking back to my father and brother maybe 10, 15, 20 miles a day. Every night I would stop at a farmer's house and knock on the door, and when I walked in, I used to say in Polish, May Jesus be blessed, and they would answer, Amen.

Now, I would also like to mention that if any one of them would point out where a Jew was located, alive or dead, they would get a reward. The reward was a kilo of sugar, two pounds of sugar, or a carton of cigarettes. That is how cheap our life was.

It would be quite naive to assume that they didn't recognize that I didn't belong there—I was a Jewish city boy, and I certainly didn't look like a Polish farmer boy. But every one of them, they slept me over, fed me, gave me some bread for the road, and they said, God be with you. These were Polish Christians.

One time, one of the farmers disappeared, and I kid you not, if I say that I could taste my heart, that's how it started to beat. I thought, Oh, ho, he certainly went to get the police. But instead he came back with a jar of money and he said to me, Krakow is still far away, buy yourself a ticket, and get yourself home. Because of him, that's exactly what I was able to do.

MARK A.
Poland

HAYYEI SARAH בראשית

Laughter

We had very little time in Gusen, very little time to rest. Even on Sunday mornings when we were off, when we didn't have to go out on work details, very rarely did we just sit around and do nothing. Somebody always came around and found some work for us to do. But when we did sit around, amazingly enough we had our sense of humor.

On Friday night we used to sit around, a few boys, and I was one of them, but most of the others thought we were crazy. As we would sit and eat our rations, we used to kid around with each other—pass the challah, pass the gefilte fish. People thought, are you nuts?! Are you crazy?! Of course, we were hoping maybe next Friday night we will have the real thing and not just talk about it. But either way, you had to have a sense of humor and we did.

We even prayed whenever we had the chance. My father died in that year, so officially I was still in my first year of mourning—we didn't realize that our whole family was— that we were all mourners. But, whenever I had a chance, I got people together to say a psalm so I can say Kaddish whenever I could. When it came Rosh Hashoneh time, we were looking around for people to remember some of the special prayers for Rosh Hashoneh like Unesaneh Tokef. We had to go on hoping and have even a little sense of humor. Otherwise, well, because the people who didn't, who looked at us like we are crazy, they didn't last long. You had to have a sense of humor.

DAVID A.
Romania

Departures

I went over to an SS guard, the same SS guard who was quite nice, and I asked him, Is there any way that my brother and I can let our Mom know that we are alive and well? He just turned around, kicked me in the pants and told me to get back into the line. I got a healthy kick from him, and really didn't expect too much more, I really didn't expect any miracle from him.

A couple of days later, maybe a week later, on the morning when we were leaving, the same guard selected out of the 100, 10 people which included my brother and me. There was a pushcart there with two big wheels, with some blankets or some clothing on top of it. He started to tell us—the 10 that he took, that we should push that cart. We had no idea where we were going or what we were doing.

Suddenly, he stopped in front of the ladies camp. He handed some documents to the guard and the guard opened up, and we went in. At barrack 14 he stopped and handed me and my brother a brown paper bag—the paper bag was full of bread, German bread that they were eating, not our garbage—it must have been a pound or a kilo. Also, I don't know how much butter, sausage, and a pocket knife. He looked at his watch and said, You have 20 minutes, find your mother. We were looking, and suddenly we heard Mom's voice. Mom was a beautiful lady and suddenly we see somebody running to us—bald, with a long striped gown—we didn't recognize.

We gave her the goodies, we kissed, and the 20 minutes were gone. That's the last time I saw Mom. It's a tough sight and a tougher memory, a beautiful, beautiful woman looking like that. Until today I hear her saying—be proud of your heritage, and the last words—be proud of your name.

GEORGE G.
Hungary

VA-YETSE'

Dreams

I don't remember anything very much from the days we stayed in Dachau. I remember the day they came in and say, raus, raus, raus, and we went out and joined a line of prisoners already walking like zombies. We started to march and march and walk and walk and walk. They say that march to Bergen Belsen lasted three weeks. We stopped in many camps, too many camps. If they had food for us, they fed us; if they didn't have food anymore, we didn't have food.

We arrived in the Austrian Alps, and I saw the mountains with snow, and it was so cold. All of a sudden, the sun came out and it was so strange with the sun. It was always grey, and the forests we passed through, they were dark and miserable and cold, and now the sun is out and the sky is blue. The sun was reflecting against some letters of some camp—Ebensee, the letters said. The sun was so much reflecting on the letters that they looked like gold.

Ebensee is the only camp I remember. We passed through a lot of camps, but 50 years later, I found out that Uncle Shmuel died two months before the liberation. And this is when I passed through. We were liberated April 14 and passed through Ebensee in February, and I was staring at the sky, and I didn't even know why I was staring at the sky. For years I thought I had a hallucination—the sun and the sky and staring at the sky and the letters Ebensee reflect by the sun. I said if I tell that to people, they're gonna think I'm crazy. But I know now that what I was staring at was real. My uncle died that day in Ebensee, and he wanted for me to be there, and I was there. I was there for him because he was my favorite uncle.

Last year when I went to Yad Vashem, and I saw this monument, this greenish monument. There is a plaque in

Hebrew and in English—700 marched from Dachau to
Bergen Belsen—the dead march—only a handful arrived to
Bergen Belsen. I start to cry there. This is my march, I said,
this is where I marched.

I didn't want to believe what happened that day, and I
didn't want to believe the feelings I had that day, but that
maybe that we hallucinated, that it's not true, that it didn't
happen, that Ebensee is only in my mind. But I didn't
hallucinate it, Ebensee was real.

LAURA V.
Italy

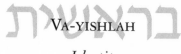

VA-YISHLAH

Identity

I was an American soldier, not a Jew. The one time I met a Jew in France was in Nancy. We had a day stopover to replenish and resupply ammunition and things, and I was walking the street. I saw this boy with a yellow star and in French it was Juif. I walked over to him and said to him in Yiddish, Bisti Yiddish? Are you Jewish?

He got scared and started to run away, but I ran after him and held him. I says, Ich bin a Yid, Ich bin a Yid, an Americanishe Yid—I am a Jew, I am a Jew, an American Jew! He looked at me and he started to cry, and I looked at that thing, the first time I'd ever seen it, you know. And with all the things that had been going on, I hadn't seen anything as dramatic as this. I asked him, Do you have to wear it? And he says, We have to wear this all of the time.

I asked him where he lived, and he said he's not living with his parents, 'cause he don't know where his parents are. And it still didn't dawn on me. He says he's living with a family, and I said, You want me to go with you? He says no, they are afraid, and I didn't know what to do. I took out some chocolates and gave him, and I noticed the number on the arm. That was the first time I noticed it, and I asked what it was. All the Jews have this.

At that moment I was called away, one of my friends said, Let's go, we got to get going. I tried to get his name, but we were off, but I'll never forget that. It was a very traumatic thing for me. We didn't know anything yet.

Until that day, I didn't know anything. I was an American soldier, not a Jew, if you follow what I'm saying. I wasn't thinking about this until I saw that star.

LESTER S.
United States

בראשית VA-YESHEV

Destiny

M y father came from a religious family. But after the death of my mother, my father became less and less religious. We wouldn't go to synagogue on Fridays any more, but we would go to my aunt's second seder, and of course Yom Kippur and Rosh Hashoneh we would go to the synagogue in town. Also, when I was in elementary school, my father brought me to religious lessons. I had to go once a week in the afternoon, which I rather liked. There we learned biblical stories and to read Hebrew and things like that. I enjoyed that.

But this is really strange. Once, when I must have been maybe 10 years old, we had to write a composition in school about the ancient Germans. We had learned they lived in forests, and they slept on bear hides, and they roasted meat and all kinds of stuff like that. And that their gods were Woltan and Thor. Suddenly, I realized that these are not my ancestors—my ancestors rode on camels in the desert. So this was some kind of an awakening. That's when I started to get a sense that Jewish was different.

Also, when I was in high school, we would go, my father and my sister and I, to the Jewish cemetery on the other side of Berlin for my mother's yahrzeit. At the cemetery we also went to the grave of my grandfather, my father's father, and there were two hands on the gravestones and I asked what that meant. My father and my sister explained to me that my father was a Kohen and that was a kind of nobility, but not to tell the children in my class, not to brag that I was of nobility or something like that because we had German nobles in class, Von Zitzewitz, and so on, but I felt good—different, but good.

IRENE A.
Germany

13

Now the camp itself was probably one of the crucial experiences of my life. We were in a vagabond camp in Belgium, but there was a judge and attorneys and bankers. I took notes in that camp, and when I went to England I wrote a book about it which I called *No Room for 600*. It was a book that was bitter—that the whole world had no room for 600 people and had to intern them in a vagabond camp in Belgium.

When I published it later, about 15 years ago, my whole concept has changed. Instead of being bitter about not having found room for the 600, I wanted to stress what 600 were able to do for themselves under the most miserable circumstances. So I called it *The Next to Final Solution* because the people in this camp, most of them, were picked up by the Nazis and shipped to Auschwitz and the Final Solution. But what was impressive was that they said we have to take things in our own hands. Otherwise, we will just rot here, nobody will take care of us. So we established a little state in this vagabond camp, a state within a state, anyway, a vagabond state.

There was a judge who wrote a constitution, I wrote a newsletter with my typewriter, and one of the most famous restaurant chefs in Vienna established the kitchen. We had classes, English classes, Spanish classes, and a cobbler class, and an auto mechanic class and all these trades that we hoped somewhere will be useful in the future. The most important thing was that everybody had a purpose—everybody either taught something or learned something. It was the greatest experience of my life to see that you can take care of your own destiny.

בראשית MIKKETS

The great lesson was you have to distinguish between areas where you have a freedom of choice and areas where you have no freedom—you have to accept what happened to you. There is no point in fighting against fate, but rather finding a meaningful attitude towards the situation which cannot be changed. But where you can change the situation you do everything you do to change it.

The best question is not, why did it happen to me, but what can I do now? And what we could do now is to prepare ourselves for the future—unfortunately it didn't work out for most of the people because the Nazis overran Belgium before most of them got out.

Early on, I still was full of rage. Why did this happen? Why doesn't the world find place for 600 people? But then later on when I really published the book—then it said this is what people did under circumstances that were really unbearable.

JOSEPH F.
Austria-Hungary

15

 Va-yiggash

Reunion

My two brothers, Benzi and Kalman, were in Mauthausen. Kalman, he didn't want to live. He always said to Benzi, let me die, let me go to our mother. But Benzi made very big effort to stay alive. When they were liberated by the Americans, both of them were very sick, very sick. The soldiers took both of them to the hospital. Benzi had meningitis, and Kalman was in the same hospital but in another place because he was even more contagious. They did not know where each other was.

One day a doctor came to Benzi and he says, Doctor, my brother is here. So the doctor said, How do you know your brother is here? Benzi said, I recognized his coughing. So the doctor thought he's hallucinating, you know, he has a high fever. But Benzi said, Doctor, I cannot die 'til I see my brother. So they found out that it really was Kalman that Benzi was hearing, and then they brought Kalman to Benzi. There wasn't a dry eye—not by the nurses, and not the doctors when the two brothers came together. Since then my two brothers, they always stuck together, they didn't leave each other for a minute.

I have such a pain in my heart that Hitler won the war against the Jews because never will I be able to be happy. On the other hand, I have a wonderful family, a wonderful family.

CILA A.
Czechoslovakia

 Va-yehi

Legacy

M y legacy and my responsibility to humanity as a survivor is this: that humanity must endeavor in some way to see that those things will never happen again anywhere in the world. Not only against the Jews, but against anyone.

I am very much disappointed that Holocausts did happen after the war in several places in the world. It seems to me that humanity did not learn anything from that experience. There was Cambodia where the Khmer Rouge killed millions of their own people, and humanity just looked and didn't stop it. There was a military regime in Argentina which killed thousands of people, taking children away from their families, and to this day many people don't know what happened to their children. Again, people around the world just looked at it and didn't stop it at all. And recently, we have the situation in Bosnia where people were killed by the thousands in exactly the Nazi style, and humanity just looked at it and talked about it. Humanity must find some way to stop this evil thing.

Humanity on this planet has the responsibility to go wherever such things are happening and stop it. Unless we develop such mechanisms, I feel very insecure in this world not only for Jews, but for all humanity. And this is the legacy I want to leave to my children and to future generations.

LEO B.
Poland

שמות EXODUS

Parenting

The headmistress at my new school in England knew my history and must have taken pity on me, taking extra special care to find what I think must have been the very best home in Kendal, that of Mr. and Mrs. Staples. I think one of the first things they did is to buy me a dog, a Chow, which is a lovely, fluffy, sheeplike animal, and I still have a picture of him.

They were Methodist, quite religious. He was the superintendent of the Sunday school and she had been a Sunday school teacher since she was 16, so our backgrounds couldn't have been more different, and yet it didn't matter at all. We just fitted together from day one.

Because of their Sunday school work they must have had a bit of psychology training, but I don't think that would have quite prepared them for me. Nevertheless that, together with their instinctive sort of good sense and the fact that they were very loving and caring, enabled them to deal with this still rather lost child from Germany. I was very much taken care of. And apart from the anxiety about my parents, in the Lake District I barely knew that there was a war on.

The Staples used to go to church every Sunday morning, but I never went with them, except on odd occasions—if there was somebody particularly interesting preaching, I would go along— maybe sort of two or three times a year. I used to go to the socials which were held there—but that's all. In fact, they didn't try to influence me religiously in the slightest—no, never, it never crossed their minds.

But I fasted for Yom Kippur and Mildred decided, announcing that fasting wouldn't do her any harm, that she would fast with me. That's the sort of people they were. I mean, they were lovely, just lovely.

RUTH B.
Germany

Liberators

I didn't know that much about concentration camps— other than the general thing that Hitler had these camps and was trying to eliminate the Jewish people. Word gets around the army, and probably from the *Stars and Stripes* newspaper. We used to get that even during the battles and all. But I didn't really know that much about them until I actually went into them.

That was in '44. I didn't know we were going into one until we drove up the road and started going through dead bodies getting into the road. They were on the outside of the camp lying on the ground.

I knew what it was. I knew what it was real quicklike. And, of course, word got down the line real quicklike where we were going into. There were bodies stacked alongside of the road, and we were in a few of the trucks that followed the tank column.

I was on the back of a tank at that time, and we began to see these bodies alongside of the road. We just went into a complete mess when we got in there—the minute we got in there—it was just a complete mess. I mean, we got sick right away, we all got sick.

There was all these Quonset huts all the way up and down the line, and they were full of dead people and live people in the same beds, and people were laying around, some of them dead and some of them alive. I'd never seen a skeleton walk before, but I saw some of them then.

We had to go through the buildings and try to make sure that there wasn't anybody else in there that could shoot at us, you know, and Joe Palermo, this guy that was with me most of the time, and I went up to this one building and we heard a noise downstairs. I told him, I said, Joe, you watch the top of the stairs here, and cover me, and I'll go down, see what the noise is. I went down and there was a big SS trooper down there chopping up bodies with an axe, heads and torsos and everything else all around, and he was doing that so he could put as many bodies in the incinerator.

When I walked up on him, he just looked at me and turned around and went back to work. I walked up and took the axe out of his hand—he was crazy—he didn't know what he was doing—he had no idea—and this is the kind of things that we run into down there. And then somebody's gonna tell me it didn't happen?!

We had to clean that mess up, it was as simple as that. We did the best we could.

JACK E.
United States

23

Redemption

I was one hundred percent sure that I would survive. That's how stupid I was.

But I knew that we had to outlive Hitler. We had to outlive Hitler, and we had to tell the world that the Jewish people cannot just perish because of an animal like Hitler.

We would survive, and we would tell our story. We would bring our story to the people in the free world, the story of what was happening, because we knew that from reading alone, nobody will ever believe that such atrocities could be directed against other human beings.

We knew that Hitler was beginning to lose the war, so we felt that eventually we will have to outlive him. Just to spite him, we had to live.

We were Jews, and we were not going to give in, to give up. We had faith in the Ribbono Shel Oylam that for this He will let us survive.

NECHAMA A.
Poland

Triumph

We knew when the war was going good for the Nazis. They would give us a little better food. When the war wasn't going good for the Nazis, we got no food. We were happy to get no food. It told us something.

Now one day they caught me making a fire. There was the desert grass growing there, and we had to cook something. Sometimes we killed a few rats or something, and we had to cook it. It was my turn to take the chance. We had lookouts to warn if anybody comes, but they didn't see, and the commandant came. He says, Fire. I said, What fire? He says, Aren't you cooking something? I said, I'm not cooking anything. He says, You are going to get it. You are never coming out of punishment camp.

The guys heard that, and I was already a skeleton to begin with, already half in the other world, and they turned around to the Commandant and said, He's not going any place, he's staying right here. The whole camp assembled at the gate, and that was the only uprising we ever had in the camp. Over me.

The commandant was going to teach us a lesson. Blood is going to flow, he says. We said that's alright, we gonna die anyway, how long you think we can hold out in this camp here? We had rocks, and the blood was flowing, believe me. Some of us died. A lot of them died. We licked our wounds, and they licked theirs, and we had no food for about three days. We didn't care.

HARRY A.
Germany

שמות YITRO

Community

I had a great childhood, not rich, far from it, lower middle class. I mean we always had something to eat on the table. My father was a tailor. He worked very hard. I was the best-dressed kid in the neighborhood because I had three or four suits every year. But the reason I'm saying I was very fortunate, because there was a woman in France, an aunt of the Rothschilds—her name was Madame Alfant—she built a seven-story high apartment house in the most magnificent section of Paris. Right in the center of Paris—there are two islands—one is called Ile de la Cité where the Cathedral Notre Dame is erected, and the other one is a smaller island called Ile Saint Louis, and on that island this remarkable woman built a seven-story high apartment house for Jewish families with lots of children who could not afford to pay rent. And it was marvelous. This seven-story apartment house was filled with children and it was joyous.

What was fantastic in our apartment house, this Madame Alfant not only didn't care if we pay the rent, and I'm sure some of the families could not afford it, they didn't pay, but she hired social workers to take care of the children when we came back from school from 4:00PM until 7:00PM. There was a, we called it a locale on the first floor—two huge rooms where the kids will go there to do their homework and then be taken care of by these social workers who were remarkable ladies. They were all in their late teens, and remarkably all these young ladies in '38 and '39 went to Israel, to Palestine, and stayed there. We had one woman who we always knew as "Lou" and she emigrated to Palestine in 1939. I never knew her last name. Later, I found out her last name, Lou Kaddar, and in Israel she became Golda Meir's private secretary and companion until Golda Meir died.

26

They were all great ladies. They would take care of us.
They would teach us the Bible. They would see to it that
we'll become good human beings. Not only our parents were
decent people, most of them, but they helped us to really
have a great life. And I think about it. Why did I survive the
Holocaust? Why me, except for a lot of people. I think what
helped me tremendously—it's my background—even though
I am not a religious person right now, but I had that
background of religion. I knew all about what it means to be
a Jew—but I had that kindness—that love—that my mother
gave us and even my father in his way because he was so busy
working and making money—but he helped us to such a
wonderful life and these ladies who taught us what's good
about life. And I had all these memories while I was
suffering. That was good and that was the balance that kept
me alive. I was young and healthy and that helped me a lot.
When I think of that childhood, it was remarkable, really
fantastic. Lots of children.

ROBERT C.
France

27

MISHPATIM

Justice

We were liberated by the Soviet army. In fact, we entered Lida with the army together, July 8th of 1944. Our partisan group was not dismissed yet—we still had things to do and I found myself escorting a convoy of prisoners of war. We gathered up 700 Vlasovtsky, the Russian collaborators with the Germans, and about 400 Germans, including officers and the last scrapings of the barrel, little kids, 15 year old boys, and we were to take them from Lida to Novogrudok, 50 kilometers away.

I think about 15 people, maybe less than 15, were escorting about 1100. They didn't dare to make a move, they were so depressed and so completely out of it. I was more afraid of the Russians than the Germans at that point because, as I said, the Germans were totally depressed.

We stopped with them once overnight in a glassworks—in the barn of a glassworks. We packed them in. I don't know how they got in, they must have slept one on top of the other because that place no way could have held 1100 people lying down—and so it was.

I thought of revenge then but, I'm ashamed to say, that I could not have brought myself to do anything because I saw—not even conquered is the right word—a beaten down people, all the men and young boys, the dregs. These people didn't hurt me, why should I hurt them? It's enough that they'll be in a prisoners of war camp—but I didn't think I could pick up a rifle and kill any of them.

I didn't feel sorry, but I couldn't do them any harm either.

BELLA G.
Poland

TERUMAH

Sacred Space

It's very hard to describe the Great Synagogue of Copenhagen. But to me, as a kid, it was huge. It was just beautiful. The Aron Hakodesh, which is where the Torah is placed, was made out of what looked to me like gold, and it spread through the entire width of the room. It was a huge hall that would house in excess of 1,000 people. And it was just beautifully furnished and maintained.

From time to time, the royalty would visit for special events. When the synagogue was 100 years old, they had a big festive affair, and King Christian came to the synagogue. So you can just imagine it was just a beautiful shul, and it still stands the same way today.

I think families that were more prominent than others would have their own pews, the smaller ones where they could just have one family sitting in it. And I remember the cantor and his family would have a separate pew so that we would sit next to my father when he was not officiating. When he was officiating, of course, he was up there, at the Omud, that's the name of it, the place where the cantor stands and sings. But we always knew that we had a place.

And the other thing I remember about the synagogue is that they were very kind to children. As a kid, 7, 8, 9 years old, whatever age it was, in the synagogue there was a candy man who would always distribute candies to the children. That was nice.

GUSTAV G.
Czechoslovakia

TETSAVVEH

Service

My life in Sopot was absolutely wonderful when I was a little girl 'cause my whole life was singing. Yossele Rosenblatt's recordings were like food in our house. And singing hazones, like a cantor, was just my dream. Of course, a girl's dreams were very much shattered in those days. In 1930, you never heard of a girl wanting to do hazones on the bimah.

So I figured out a way. In the synagogue there are two tiers: the women sit upstairs and the men downstairs. But the choir, the boys' choir, was upstairs. The upstairs was made in the synagogue like a "u," going all around, and the bimah was in the center. The Hazan would look up and signal the boys' choir.

I decided I was gonna sit on the right, not next to my mother, but opposite the choir on that "u," so he would hear me from one side and the boys' choir from the other side. And I harmonized. And I used to drive him meshugeh. Really nuts. So after a couple of months of this, he decided to talk to me and decided to talk to my parents. He said if I cut my braids, make my hair very short, he would stick me into the boys' choir. And that's exactly what happened.

In America, we were able to buy a house in Oceanside. I became very involved with singing again in the synagogue and doing everything in shul. As my kids, who we taught about the importance of education, got older, they said, How about you Mom? You should go to Hebrew Union. I wanted to be a hazante, a lady hazan. I mean it might sound crazy, but I wanted to be a hazante from early days in my childhood.

I applied to Hebrew Union, and I remember the answer from the director like he would be sitting here. He says,

You're about 20 years too early. Maybe in 20 years from now they will accept women. Little did he know what he said. Because 19 1/2 years later the first woman was graduated from that school!

BETTY R.
Greece

Ki Tissa'

Hope

Dirnau was my first labor camp after Birkenau. I remember working in the tunnel. Fortunately, I was together with my rebbe who used to teach me in cheder. He shared his rations with me. He said, I am not going to survive. I'm sure I'm not going to survive, but I can assure you, you will survive, and he gave me strength. He shared his rations with me.

He told me the importance of life and he said that when you survive, remember the difference between a Torah life and a non-Torah life. I remember his teaching about human dignity, about the importance of being kind, compassionate, the way we are supposed to respect every human being. He used to tell us stories about the way the rabbis used to get up for gentiles, old gentiles. Even though it was for a gentile, the rabbi used to get up because the gentile had more experience in life. He tried to encourage me not to give up hope and instill in me the love of God, that's what I remember.

When I was separated from him, I used to think back on the way he encouraged me and the way he blessed me. That was so important to me. I took it very seriously. I tried my best in every circumstance to think positive. And if I saw danger I would try to escape from it. It's because of his encouragement that I feel I survived.

Moses K.
Romania

ויקהל VA-YAKHEL

Refuge

They put us on little trucks through the forest to the camp in Flossenberg. I was on the last truck with a friend of mine, and when all the trucks started to move already, I and Sheyndl Goldman, we jumped off the truck. So for one night we were free, a night and a day, walking around, sick and filthy and with the lice, afraid anybody should see us because we did not look like humans. We really looked like something from the other world.

And I said to her, You know Sheyndele, we have to get some food. So where do you go get food? I said, You know, let's go in the cemetery and she and I went in the cemetery, and we started to cry, and we started to scream on the graves of these people. I said, Please, dear God, open up your ears, just listen to us, just for a little while, just listen to us and help us, is that so much to ask? I'm talking to Him, but nothing happened. His eyes were stuffed, His ears were stuffed, nothing worked, nothing, He turned His head totally.

We picked ourselves up and I said, You know we still have to get some food. So food you can get only in a house. When we saw the first house, I knocked at the door and a beautiful lady opens up the door, white, with a white apron, I remember so well. I said, Good evening, in German, and said, We are hungry.

So, she looked at us and she sees the things, the lice. She wouldn't let us in. And then she said, But how can I leave you children alone? So you know, she took us in and she gave us food. And she gave us underwear to change. And she asked if we want to sleep there, but I was afraid to stay.

We left the house at about 12 o'clock, and we said good night. We took the extra food she gave us, and we went back to the cemetery to sit in peace and eat up our food.

MILA B.
Poland

33

שמות PEKUDEI

Success

J a, I've had a good life in the U.S. I have two children, they both made college. I also worked until I was 81 years old, and if the store wouldn't have closed up, I might be still working now.

I was here in America three days and I worked already. After seventeen years working for someone else in the business, I opened my own business, a furniture store on West End Avenue. I went to all the manufacturers, American Heritage, Bassett, you name it. They said, you take whatever you want and you pay whenever you can.

I had a good name. It made me so proud. Ja, I've had a good life in the U.S.

HERBERT A.
Germany

LEVITICUS

ויקרא

Sacrifice

W e did not hear about births or funerals in the ghetto. My friends and I would talk about what happens when the war is over. Do we go back to school? Do we get married? Do we have children? The only thing we could do in the ghetto is dream. And unless you would have a dream, you wouldn't have made it, you really wouldn't have made it. You just had to feel that you're going to make it—that you want to be part of the living instead of part of the dead. But, in '42, it got very bad.

I remember my aunt became pregnant, and she didn't want to give birth to the child. She found somebody that would abort the baby. But she didn't want to say anything to my Mom because my Mom would say, How could you? She asked my sister to go with her for the abortion and my sister said, I can't do it. So I went with her instead.

But in the ghetto, there was no anesthesia. So I was standing there holding her head and holding her hand. Now that was a horror to witness. But giving birth would have been much worse. It was horrible. But we stuck together, did for each other; we were a family.

SOPHIE R.
Poland

37

 TSAV

Giving

What did it mean to have a camp friend? Well, what it always means to have a good friend. But maybe it meant more, you know, because friendship in bad times is more valuable than friendship in good times. This is because, as friends, we help each other and it's easier to be friendly in good times. In bad times, that's another story because it often takes sacrifices. You see, friends would give moral support when we felt low, when we felt like giving up.

I remember distinctly, there was a moment when we thought that they were going to kill us all—this was later, after the Schindler's camp and after Auschwitz, in the last camp where they liberated me. There was a moment that everybody thought that this is the end.

Now usually I felt strong and my friends believed in me, so they asked me, Will we live through this? Again, because I always believed, I always said yes, we will live through. Then one of my friends, she said again, So what do you think Ada, will we really live through? And that was the one time, and the first time, that I really doubted. But I didn't want to show her my doubt, so I said, What are you asking me, am I God or something?

I was strong for my friend in that camp and, from that camp, we were liberated.

ADA A.
Poland

SHEMINI

Eating

Iremember the first, very first month after the war, lots of Jewish soldiers from Lithuania that were in the Russian army were passing by and would stop at our apartment. They were given a leave of absence from the army for a couple days to try to find their families, their relatives. So they would camp in our apartment and bring a little bit of food that they were given for their two or three days' leave. They were sleeping at our apartment on tables at night, and Mom would cook meals for them.

I remember that from this, my mother was able to buy for me the first egg in my life. I refused to eat it. I didn't know what it was, so I said I don't eat this food. I need something that I was used to eating in the ghetto.

I also remember the first few years after the war, in the evening, we used to sit at the table, and Mom would give me a slice of bread and a little piece of sausage. I was trying to eat it, but she wouldn't let me. She said no, you cannot eat it yet. First, you have to wrap the bread with the sausage and you will finish eating the bread alone. Then you will eat the sausage. The bread had to have the taste like you ate it with the sausage, because Russian soldiers were not bringing in sausage. Mom could only buy a little piece from the Lithuanians. It was very precious. So this was our way with food.

ASKIVA F.
Lithuania

Sexuality

Since my husband already had lived for quite a while in Westerbork, he had his own bedroom that he shared with other people, about six people altogether. I saw that bedroom only once and that was when we were married one year. He asked the other guys to stay out of the room so that he could be together with me, and they stayed away.

He had managed to put a flower there, and he managed to give me a piece of jewelry which was made for me. It was a brooch from silver, shaped like an R for Renee. It was all polished—it was beautiful—so a jeweler had made that for my husband in Westerbork which was already a camp, and he gave it to me there in that room with the one rose on the table. I looked at the back of the brooch and there was only a safety pin connected with it—not a real professional safety lock, but I managed to wear it when I arrived in Auschwitz.

So we were in bed for the first time in Westerbork and there was a knock, knock. Who is knocking the door? He had all arranged to be free, but there stood my mother and she said, congratulations. She came with a cake that she baked from old bread—rebaked something. My husband didn't know how to express himself but he was mad inside of him, but I didn't insult her. After five minutes, he said to her, Please would you go away now because this is the only time, the first time, that I am with my wife, and she left with crying and tears over her cheeks.

Then he was trying to make love to me, and I could not make love to him like he expected. I was so hurt from the situation we were in that if he did make love to me, I don't remember any beauty of it. I remember only that it was destruction rather than a celebration.

Then he tried to make love to me one more time when he had me close. That was in the train to Auschwitz. It was so noisy in the train from the wheels underneath that he said I shouldn't have to worry. We won't make noise, he said. But all of a sudden I did hear his shoes on the floor, and he hurt me so much that I was sick for a long time afterward. And he said to me this is the last time in my life, in his life. That was true. That was my married life.

RENEE D.
Germany

METSORA'

Healing

In 1941, I got dysentery—there was an epidemic of dysentery in Lodz, and I also got it. My auntie was cooking the liquid from rice, was giving me to drink, but I got weaker and weaker and thinner and thinner. I thought this was the end of me. But we had a doctor who was a relative of ours in Lodz ghetto. I remember he was shaking the head telling mother it's very difficult now to recover from this, but he said I will try to get injection.

He brought me this injection which was a serum against dysentery. This injection was designed only for VIPs in ghetto. It was a horse serum. He gave me this injection and what happened after one or two days was terrible. I became swollen, and the next day I became paralyzed, not able to talk. Seeing everything, understanding everything, but not able to communicate with anybody. The whole family was convinced that I am dying. The doctor said now I can't do anything anymore to him, I gave him the injection, but I gave it too late.

Maybe a week later, I see they're putting big candles on, lighting the candles, and people are coming with prayer shawls, and starting to pray, but I can't say anything. So I thought that they're going to bury me alive. They think that I am dead because I can't speak, I can't move, I can't communicate. I'm lying like a piece of wood on the bed, so I was really thinking then that they're going to bury me alive which was possible in ghetto.

But what happened after that, they left, but the candles were still on. I was lying in bed thinking that they're waiting for the candles to go out before burying me. But they didn't bury me. It took another week, but I started to move, I started to talk, and they were feeding me with rice, but I needed more protein to recover.

What happened was, we had a chicken that was sleeping in the corner with me, and suddenly the chicken started to lay eggs! So we put a little bit of straw that she could lay eggs. Every day she lay an egg for me, every day. And this chicken saved my life by laying an egg every day, giving me the protein.

So eventually I recovered from this, thanks to the chicken. When the chicken died—they told me to say prayers for dead people—the kaddish—for the chicken which saved my life.

ADAM K.
Poland

43

'AHAREI MOT

Atonement

A t the end of the war, Schwerin was going to be given
up by the Americans to the Russians and they didn't
care about what would happen there. I was
dominated by the need to get the hatred out of my system—
to do something to avenge myself. So with a few other guys
we formed a command of the city because we wanted to have
revenge on them Germans. We made a German printer print
a proclamation to the German population where we said,
You're not allowed on the streets for the next three weeks. If
you have to go out and you are attacked by anybody then you
can yell three times, Hilfe, hilfe, hilfe—help, help, help, and
then pray to your God.

We also found bunkers in the middle of the city with
about 70 to 80 rooms underground, containing the archives
of the National Socialist Party and some of their treasures—a
lot of valuables and books with signatures by Hitler.
Although we hated them so much that we burned it all. We
dynamited it and burned it. Then we went to the railway
station in Schwerin, and there were whole trains full of newly
printed German money and American money because they
falsified American dollars, millions of them.

The stationmaster was in terror that we're going to kill
him, and he led us to it. He said, Look, there's so much
money, you just get this and you will be all right for life, you
know, millions and millions of American dollars. But what
we did, because we were full of hatred and couldn't think
about getting any advantage, any profit out of this—we were
all boiling, you know, with hate — so we burned all this
money and all this railway station. We burned half of
Schwerin really.

'AHAREI MOT

But my greatest satisfaction was that I was instrumental in getting justice for the greatest Nazi war criminal, Kaltenbrunner, the chief of the Gestapo. Kaltenbrunner denied everything, absolutely everything. He said, Yes I was in the office—I was signing papers, but I never touched a prisoner, I never touched anybody. I was the only prisoner who could say I saw him watching every extermination in the gas chamber. That was my greatest satisfaction.

JERZY B.
Sweden

KEDOSHIM

Love

So, then the kapos came screaming, Heraus, heraus, heraus—go, go, go, leave everything, you will get it later, you will get it later.

We were going down from the wagon and it was mother, my sister-in-law, Nuzhi, me and Buzhi. A kapo came to my sister — Nuzhi was a beautiful, beautiful girl—and took out from her hands the baby, put it in my mother's hand, and took her a few rows in front, on the side, where the young people were going.

Suddenly, there was my brother, who saw how it's going because a man was standing there. He saw what was going on. He called to Nuzhi, and right away she took back the baby and, as she did, she came back. And when they arrived, my mother and her, they went one side but my sister Buzhi and me, we went on the other side. Later on, I find out that my brother on our side went over on the other side to protect my mother and my sister with the baby.

I never knew that I will never see her again. If I would have known, believe me, that I would have gone to the other side, too.

After that, I was always together with my sister and my friend. We took the name of Sabul, all three of us, that we should be always together. When we had this little water for washing, for what I was fighting ferociously, and so it was—one day, one wash herself up, the first one, and the second one and the third one, and lower body, one first, and the next day the next one was the first one, and so we were just to each other.

CLARA R.
Hungary

 'EMOR

Sacred Time

Nobody believed it would take so long to get free. I mean every day was like a year then. It was just hell. I don't know how you survive if you wouldn't have the faith in God, if you wouldn't have the faith that tomorrow it would already be over. It was like a struggle every day just to get up from the bed. Just to wash in the morning was so cold and just a little water was coming up. The water was freezing—not cold—ice—yeah, it was just hell there, hell.

But we knew, we knew what holiday it was. I don't know how, but we knew everything, maybe a calendar or whatever. I don't know. For example, when I knew it came to Kol Nidre, I put on something nicer. Also, I was working with Rebbetzin Halberstadt on Yom Kippur when I saw the machines breaking. I would come down, and I would say look at what happened. I will fix it. But she wouldn't let me. She says, It's yontef today, I do it—you're not doing for me. She says thank you for seeing it, but she wouldn't let me fix it. She says I'm going to do it myself, the rebbetzin who was davening every day. It was Yom Kippur for everybody.

ETA B.
Poland

47

Liberation

Toward the end, the Germans, the soldiers, are saying, You know the Americans are coming in and we want to protect you—we want to take you to the tunnel for protection, and naturally the kapos was telling us, No, no, no, don't go in.

And naturally we didn't go in because the purpose was to take us to the tunnel to blow up the tunnel. To blow up the people, that was the whole idea.

So finally after some days, the American tanks rolled in and that was—it was a day of miracles.

I felt, again, a human being. Right away. I felt that, that I am free. I felt that the whole world is mine. At the moment of liberation, that moment, I felt the whole world was mine.

GABOR A.
Hungary

BE-HUKKOTAI

Obligation

I was just fifteen years old when World War II broke out. While six million Jews were murdered and millions more endured indescribable suffering, many Europeans chose to remain blind, deaf, and dumb to the plight of their Jewish neighbors. As a nation, we felt abandoned by God and by people.

A peasant farmer named Sidor courageously stood up in the face of injustice and changed the world. He was the poorest of the village and too uneducated to even sign his own name, but his heroism, values, and strength of character far transcended our small town.

Sidor saved my life, and my family, from the hand of Nazi execution. He risked his own life, and those of his wife and only daughter, knowing there would be no monetary reward for his sacrifice. Despite the grave dangers, Sidor offered my parents, my little brother, and me a place of refuge: a tiny dugout under his chicken coop. For nearly two and a half years, the four of us hid there, in a crouching position, totally dependent on Sidor for food, water, and disposal of our waste. Each footstep we heard brought the renewed threat of discovery, and of death.

Sidor shared with us his last morsel of bread, even when he did not have enough to sustain his family, even when he knew that helping a Jew was punishable by death. When he caught typhus from us, he refused to seek medical attention for fear of jeopardizing our security. Doctors knew that it was the Jews in hiding who had lice, and lice were the carriers of this disease.

Sidor never did explain his deep resolve to help us survive. He was simply a good Christian with no ulterior motives who saw it as his duty to save another human life. We were Jews, and he was Christian, but we were all human beings.

FANYA G. H.
Poland

במדבר NUMBERS

בְּמִדְבַּר BE-MIDBAR

Home

When I was a little boy five, six, seven years old, I used to go to my grandparents—to my father's parents. My zeyde, Mordechai, had nine children and Friday night we used to go there and twice a year yontef, that was Shavuos and Simchas Torah, was the two holidays when we came in. Anyways, Friday night all the children came home to his house before returning to their own homes, and he used to bless them.

He was a short man, you know, but they just bent down to him that he shouldn't even reach, that they just shouldn't be too high, and kissed the hand. And then over to my Bube Ruhel and kissed her hand. After that, they went home to their own families. But they all had to come to say good Shabbos or good yontef to them first. That's where I've seen what respect means. They were all grown up people, all were business men, but the respect was there.

The same with my mother's parents who lived in Klausenberg—I went there and they always wanted to know what I learned. That Zeyde, he always used to give me a— they call it Shabes-oyps—a special treat for Shabbos, a fruit or a piece of kishke, and I kissed his hand, too. That's how we learned what it means to have a home.

AKIVA YOSSEF M.
Romania

Blessing

I repeated the 91st psalm in the Hebrew which now, I remember only part of it—and when it came to the part, "I gave my angels charge over thee, to watch over thee in all your travels," so I thought that the angels are carrying me. It's hard. I can't have the feeling now what I had then. I haven't got even the faith now which I had then.

Now I believe in the great architect of the universe, and I know all this outward worship got no meaning whatsoever. When we pray, we pray to ourself. Not for ourself, to ourself, which makes it much easier to overcome whatever problem there is. I don't believe in an anthropomorphical God—God is not man. I believe a part which is written, that God created man in His image and likeness—so that means I go to the mirror, I see myself. So God goes to His mirror, He sees me. I am His.

It helped me a lot to know this, that I'm part of the universe. There were times where I couldn't sleep and then I thought—well, Edward, lay down, imagine that you are lying down on the globe and you turn together with the globe, and I fell asleep. Counting sheep didn't help. But this helped. Even now I think, oh well, I close my eyes, lay down and how a globe is turning and I am turning with it. I fall asleep.

EDWARD R.
Poland

בהעלתך
BE-HA'ALOTEKHA

Starting Over

In August of '46, I was already pregnant with my first child. I was 17 at the time, and this was in the American zone, so we were able to take a train to a place called Kaltersee. We came in there, a DP camp, and talked to a woman who was working for UNRWA (United Nations Relief Works Agency), and we started to cry. She gave us a room, and we stayed there three years.

Then we came to America, which was also difficult, because the Polish quota was very difficult, so you had to wait. But then Truman took off the quota, and we had papers to come from the family—my husband's family.

Oh, it was wonderful. I remember arriving on April 24, 1949. We arrived in Boston harbor. It was still dark, and I went on the deck, and I looked out to Boston with all the lights—I said, Isn't it wonderful? It looks like paradise.

But they didn't let us down from the boat until daytime. You know, the tug boats come and pull you in. Then my husband's family came to pick us up and they took us to their home, and they were wonderful to us. They got us an apartment, and my husband started working for them—The Style Finish Company, and we all lived together.

Is there a message in all this? Well, it was meant to be, that I should live through this horrible war, come to America, and have my wonderful children that I love very much.

RUTH A.
Poland

שלח לך SHELAH LEKHA

Self-Confidence

A t about one o'clock in the morning, the boxcar doors were flung open to the roaring of guards and the braying of dogs. We were entering Buchenwald camp, but we didn't know that. We were hustled out into the night, searchlights playing on the ranks. There must have been 1,000 people by that time and we were marched through the military portion of the camp, which was a beautifully organized place with villas on each side, toward a medieval looking gateway. In the light of the searchlights we saw the motto of the camp emblazoned in brass letters above the gateway. It said, Recht oder unrecht, mein vaterland.

You know if you read today about concentration camps, you learn that many of them had as a motto, arbeit macht freude— a work is joy, or Arbeit macht frei—it makes free. That was not in this camp. In this camp, it said, Recht oder unrecht, mein vaterland—right or wrong, my country. And as I saw that, I thought that was a devastatingly German way of looking at it. But I learned much later that it wasn't a German statement at all, but it was an American statement translated into German.

In the Revolutionary War, Stephen Decatur, a naval officer, lifted his glass to his fellow officers and he said, My country, may she always be right, but right or wrong, my country— Recht oder unrecht, mein vaterland, thereby issuing one of the most immoral statements ever made, where patriotism takes the first seat and your own sense of what is right and wrong disappears. It was such a bad statement that the Germans thought it ideal as the motto of a concentration camp.

REIDAR D.
Norway

Resistance

Every Norwegian is a Lutheran whether he wants to be a Lutheran or not because there is a Norwegian Lutheran state church. We boys were part of the young people's Christian movement, the YMCA. The YMCA in Norway is an evangelical organization. It had nothing to do with sports. There are no YMCA houses that have swimming pools and tennis courts and that sort of thing. At the YMCA, we had meetings and prayer meetings and all in all the YMCA was a spiritually very, very active organization that helped us a lot in times of trouble.

For instance, in the big school recess, the half hour break at midday, we would sit in the park and when the Germans came by we would whistle "The Stars and Stripes Forever" and we would watch the Germans fall into rhythm from this totally prohibited piece of music. We would do other little things. We would wear a paper clip in our lapel that meant that we stick together. When we saw somebody with a paper clip in his lapel, we were sure that he was on our side. It became so annoying to the Germans and to the Nazis that they sent out a decree and said subject to imprisonment is he who wears a paper clip in his lapel and we thought that we had accomplished something by having this one law being passed.

We still continued to wear paper clips, of course, and Quisling sent his men in uniform, local Norwegian supporters of the Nazis, out to remove the paper clips from our lapels. But then in the underground paper, we were told to put a razor blade behind the paper clip. The young Nazis would come and pick up the paper clips, and so there were lots of bloody hands in my hometown at that particular time and throughout Norway because this spread like wildfire

throughout the country. We felt good every time we did something that would displease the occupation forces or their hench people who were the local Nazis.

REIDAR D.
Norway

במדבר HUKKAT

Continuity

They began to gather up Jews and take them away. My parents felt that they had to see if they could somehow save the family, and the first thing that they wanted to do is see if they could save the children. Since I was the youngest, I think that they made the decision that they would try to save me first.

They did explain to me what was happening, that the Germans were taking families, and they didn't know what was happening to them but they knew they were taking them away, and it was very, very frightening. So they felt that by hiding me I had a better chance of surviving. They found a place in a sanatorium, a TB sanatorium in Brussels where the directress of the sanatorium was very supportive of trying to hide Jewish children.

I remember being taken there and I remember having a very, very difficult adjustment.

And my parents, who had brought me there, they said they would come back and visit.

When they came, I think I spent most of the time just enjoying the fact they were visiting and taking in their presence as much as possible, and just hoping that things would end and I could go back to being a normal child, but it didn't work out.

The last visit occurred sometime in either December or early January of 1942, '43—it was a bitter cold day. My parents came to visit with my sisters—and they brought me a basket with all kinds of cookies and candy and things like that and the basket had a lock on it. When they were leaving, I took it. After the visit I realized that the lock was broken, so I ran after them.

It was very cold out, and when I get cold, my lips dry, and

my lips split, and my nose was bleeding, and I was crying. I ran and I got to the gate. It was a long, long drive, and I got to the gate just as they were leaving, and so they came back. My sister remembers that when she turned around I was looking, I was holding onto the bars of the gate and she saw my face through it, and she said it just broke her heart. They came back and my mother kissed me and said, Don't worry, we'll bring you a new basket next time, it's not a problem. And that was the last time I saw them. I was seven.

CHARLES R.
Belgium

במדבר BALAK

Faith

I'm coming from a very religious family, and our faith was our God. We believed in God, and tefillin come into the place, into camp. We lined up in the morning to put this tefillin on, to say the bracha. It went on for a few days, a few weeks, very religious old rabbis, we as the believers, me and my brother was there with them, and somebody told the SS what's going on.

One beautiful morning they come with machine guns and machine gunned the whole lot of us off. Me and my brother escaped and a few others. All the other guys got killed there. Now I ask God, or whatever you want, why those people deserved that at the time they were praying to God.

Now from there on, from there on I am an atheist. I don't believe in God. I don't believe in anything. If God could do that to us at the time, as far as I'm concerned it's non-existent. I firmly believe that God is non-existent.

FRANCIS JOSEPH P.
Hungary

PINHAS

Restitution

When Annie and me got married and our Lillian was born, our youngest one, in 1951, I was still very, very isolated. I couldn't just discuss things, and I never talked to Annie about it in the early years. Matter of fact, in '55 she came in one day from work and she said, You know, I read in the papers that you can claim compensation from the German government, restitution. But I didn't want it. I put a solid wall up against it. I couldn't bear even to talk about it at that time, and that's the way I felt right 'til 1992.

In 1992 our Lillian met a couple who started talking to her, and the gentleman was born in Poland and he was in Auschwitz—had similar experiences to myself, but at a lot younger age. He was telling her about it and he asked Lillian whether I was getting a pension—as he had been getting for over 20 years. Lillian says no.

When you get home, get your father to ring me, he says. So I phoned him, and we had a long chat, and he supplied me with the phone number of a gentleman who he feels would be able to help me. So I rang up, introduced myself, and he says in a very strong German accent, What then is it you want from me? I says, Well, I'm wondering whether you can advise me, to see whether I can get a pension, as other people been getting. He said, Where the hell you been the last 40 years? I says, I beg your pardon. He said, You're Jewish aren't you? I says, I am. He said, Where you been the past 40 years? I says, I don't understand your question, I've been working for Marks and Spencer all of my life. He said, Well, if you work for Marks and Spencer you don't want any money, you get a good pension. I says, Thank you for your help, sorry I bothered you. And I just put the phone down and was very, very upset.

The next morning our daughter Lillian phoned the
German embassy in London, who then gave her a full address
for the Claims Conference in Frankfurt. So we wrote a letter
then, but then I didn't heard anything for about 18 months.
Then, in July 1995, out of the blue, a letter arrives from the
Claims Conference: Very pleased to inform you that the
German government has decided to pay one lump payment of
1500 marks, so I've been getting my pension.

But it's not just for the money's sake, it's just to....You see,
when that letter came and said that I qualified to receive this
pension, that's the first time after all these years, after all
these years, that I'm getting a piece of paper which admits
the Germans did wrong, that I got an identity, which I
always had within myself, of what happened to me. People
should know.

EUGENE B.
Czechoslovakia

במדבר MATTOT

Speaking

I remember entire Saturdays and Sundays when my mother did nothing else except sit in a chair and was praying and crying. She was not a religious person, but you see, the Hungarian women had a prayer book called the Miriam prayer book. It had translations and summaries of major Jewish prayers in there, important prayers, all in Hungarian. My mother and God had long conversations in those days.

Later, we're on this train, and the train—I could read by then, and I read on the train that it said: eight horses or 40 people. It was a boxcar. It wasn't like a Pullman car. It was a boxcar—eight horses or 40 people. But they put 120 of us into that train. You couldn't do anything else but stand or crouch—even sitting took up too much room. Eventually, the train started moving and they gave us two buckets—one was a bucket for bathroom, the other one was an empty bucket that they were going to put food in.

The train went to Budapest and the way we knew we were in Budapest was that we passed by the zoo, and I happened to see the animals. The other kids in the train all came up front to the door, and we looked at the elephant and giraffe, and then we just went on, on and on. I kept asking my mother if this is the time when they're going to take us to be killed. My mother said, No. I said, How do you know? She says, Just shut up and pray. For my mother, the answer for everything was pray.

PETER C.
Hungary

בְּמִדְבַּר MASE'EI

Protection

The last seven months of the war, when we were under Oskar Schindler's care and under Mrs. Emily Schindler's care, we were well protected. In that time, hundreds and thousands of the Jewish people, all my family, all my friends—they were sent on death marches where 90 percent of them died, they froze to death, they died of starvation, they died by the bullets, but not us.

When we went to work for Oskar Schindler it was like going to heaven. We were away from Amon Goeth, we were away from all the killing. At Oskar Schindler's camp we had more food, we had barracks that were warmer in winter, and in summer when it was very hot, we were allowed to sleep outside.

But when the war was ending, Oskar Schindler called us to the factory to announce that the war was going to end at midnight, and we listened to the broadcast by Winston Churchill on the BBC. Now he had to leave. Mr. Schindler knew we were going to be liberated by the Russians, and he had to give himself up to the Americans because the Russians would shoot him as a war criminal, so we had to say goodbye. We all went by in a line and kissed his hand, Oskar's hand, and Mrs. Schindler's hand, and we all cried. I cried, and I felt like my father was being taken away again. Here I was supposedly going to be liberated, but I was afraid.

Oskar Schindler was wonderful. He was handsome, very handsome, well dressed and just looking at him made you feel good, made you feel hopeful. He made us feel that he cared about us and he wanted to help us and he wanted to feed us, that he would fight for us if the Germans wanted to kill us. He was just wonderful. I felt safe, I felt safe, I felt protected. We all did.

RENA F.
Poland

DEUTERONOMY דברים

DEVARIM

Courage

I want to tell about the hanging parties. The hanging parties were where they invited everyone to come from outside the camp to see the hanging, and they made benches ready for them to sit. They came with cars, motorcycles, horses and wagons, thousands of them, and they watched. The SS man said that this group was going to be hanged because they run away—that was the famous thing. But the crowd, the Germans, hollered, Hang them murderers—kill the Jews, kill them, shoot them. And they spit on us.

This party didn't go so good for them. This one young guy, who was going to hang, asked the SS if he could tell his brothers not to run away. He let him talk—he started to say, Brothers…enough! We are not guilty, this is madness! In two minutes or three minutes we'll be going in heaven and we gonna pray—we want you to pray with us. Then he turned, he turned to the SS man and he said—he opened his mouth like he was going to say something—and he spit in his face!

He said nobody is going to hang me—then he spit in his face again, and the SS man shot him. But he wasn't hanged.

We were punished for I think two days—we didn't have no food at all—no water, nothing. But this young man had the courage—he said, Enough.

MORDECHI F.
Poland

My mother taught me behavior, how to behave properly when you see a Nazi coming towards you on the street. You have to immediately get off the sidewalk, she showed me, and she demonstrated for me exactly what to do. No eye contact, she said, do not look into his eyes, you're not allowed to do that. You have to look down, you have to put your hands behind your back, and we practiced it, we role played it.

She would walk towards me and she'd say, I'm the Nazi; I'm walking and she told me quickly to get off the sidewalk which I did, put my hand behind my back, my eyes were down like this, you know, and let him pass by. And if I wore anything on my hair I have to immediately take it off as a sign of respect, and I remember her teaching it to me, teaching it to me.

There was one woman who apparently didn't do that for whatever reason. She didn't get off the sidewalk fast enough so they had a public shooting, and I remember my mother saying to me, I'm going to take you and show you what's going to happen to you if you don't follow these rules. She was a young woman at the time—must have been in her thirties. They tied her hands to a pole, and everybody stood around, and they shot her. And my mother said, Watch. She felt that protecting me was too dangerous.

I can't imagine taking my child to a shooting, but she did and she taught me. The reason I remember so much is because she insisted on talking to me and telling me as much as possible about what's going on. She felt that ignorance is death. You have to have as much information as possible. I was four and a half at the time.

TOVA F.
Poland

 'EKEV

Devotion

We all need heroes and I guess it's the healthy part in me that makes Dr. Janusz Korczak my hero. He was a pedagogue, he was a doctor and his mission in life was loving children. His mission in life was to be a parent to orphans and he ran orphanages. I loved him— my first love was through his books. He wrote books about children and all my friends read them. I think every Polish child read them. In his books, the heroes were children and they became kings, and it was like turning tables.

Usually during the summer we would go to the country, and one year we went to a children's camp in the country. Our counselor told us about Dr. Korczak. She was an orphan, and she was raised in his orphanage. When she talked about him, she talked about her father, and we were wondering how could he be a father to so many children. She said that every time a child was sick or had a loose tooth, they always ran to Dr. Korczak because if he pulled the tooth it absolutely didn't hurt. That's the love that he imparted and the love that the children felt for him.

During the war, Dr. Korczak stayed in the ghetto with the orphanage. But the whole Polish community, the non-Jewish community, wanted to save Dr. Korczak. So they pleaded with him: save yourself. They said, You are very important, you are not an ordinary person. What will you accomplish if you die? He said, I can't leave my children.

The last that I saw of Dr. Korczak was during the liquidation of the Warsaw ghetto. An ordinance came out that the orphanage has to be delivered to Treblinka, and there was a last minute attempt to still save Dr. Korczak. He made several choices. One of his choices was staying, the other was how to do it most mercifully for the children. So what he did

71

 'EKEV

was he told the children that they are going on an outing, on a picnic. He gave them flags and, singing the Hatikvah, he marched right into the ovens of Treblinka with his children.

ESTELLE L.
Poland

# RE'EH

Celebration

When the liberation of Paris came, I knew it. I knew it. It's really something to describe when a child sees adults jump and dance and play just like children because this is exactly what happened. How I knew about it is that we all went out to the street, without any problems, without having to worry. And there were confettis of paper thrown. Everybody was laughing and all the people in the street held hands and made what we call a farandole, which means we held hands through all the streets and made a line and sang liberation songs or sang English songs like, It's a long way to Tipperary, it's a long way to go.

I was caught into it, into the joy of it, of course, but I was amazed, poor child of five, to see grown-ups behave like that. As I want you to know that in those days there was more of a generation gap between grown-ups and children. Now, grown-ups kid around with children and play with them, but I'd never seen that, I never knew that. There was a big, big gap, and that gap was completely gone on liberation day.

I remember seeing American soldiers in the streets, they were very recognizable. They had crew cuts and they were chewing gum, they had duck voices, you know. They were very friendly with kids and they were giving out chewing gum, which at that time I named cheving gum. We were waving the flag and they were waving back to us. It was some atmosphere, a very, very special atmosphere, after the war. That was 1944.

REBECCA B.
Germany

SHOFETIM

Righteousness

I remember I was sitting on the roadside somewhere up in Germany, and I was heating my C-rations over a can of Sterno, and I'm filthy and dirty, and this guy comes up in a jeep. He's clean, and he says he's from *Yank* magazine. He said, We want to take a picture of you sitting at the roadside there with your weapon and all because it's a great picture.

So they took a picture of me and he said, Let me ask you something. He says, How do you as a black soldier reconcile the fact that you're discriminated against—you're segregated against—you're treated badly and yet you fight here. What's it all about? I said, The only way I can explain this is that I guess I'm fighting for the right to fight when I get back home.

I'm sure that is one of the things that kept me going. I'm sure it was. I just kept saying, we gotta end this crazy thing. And that's the reason why since the war I've been involved with Dr. King. I think I've been in a jail in every state in the South. So I've been constantly fighting for people's rights.

Dr. King and I sat up one night in jail, and he asked me the question, Why you here boy? And I said, Dr. King, I saw what Dachau camp was, what millions of people have been through. And I said, You know something? I know what the end of bigotry looks like, what the solution to bigotry looks like from the standpoint of the bigot, okay? Those people who believe that they're better than other people and believe that solution to those other people is to destroy them, I've seen that and I don't want that to ever happen again.

Why did we fight the war in the first place? And who were we fighting? What was that about? Think about it, that one man and his followers believed that they were better than everybody else in the world—that they were Aryans. I don't

know what an Aryan is, but I heard Germans talk about the fact that they were important, they were better. But one human being can't be any better than another.

PAUL P.
United States

KI TETSE'

Memory

I was in Ravich in the penitentiary there. There were a lot of Polish guards. There we were treated a little bit better I think. In Posen, if you didn't move fast enough they hit you. In Ravich, I did not experience anything like this.

Ravich is south of Posen. The exact distance I don't know. This was the end of March—I'm sorry—the middle of November or so. It was cold. I was 19. I cannot recall how long it took to get from Posen to Ravich.

You know, there are certain things which I just blank out completely. As a matter of fact, when I started to write my book two years ago I couldn't even remember some of the camps I was in or the dates.

Slowly, by researching and by being interviewed by my co-writer, by retelling the stories, the memories came back. But for almost fifty years that was part of my life which just did not exist. I could have used Dr. Freud to explain to me how I forgot.

CURT A.
Czechoslovakia

 Kɪ Tᴀᴠᴏ'

Homecoming

When I came to this country, if I saw a person that was different from me I walked on the other side of the street. I was afraid. I was very afraid of policemen. I had fear of all kinds of people with uniforms. It was terrible. On the ship coming here, I had terrible nightmares about even coming to America.

Before we stepped off the ship, though, I put on the only dress I had. It was a sailor dress, a two piece. We got dressed in our best when we started to see the Statue of Liberty because we knew this was freedom.

We knew because this was a ten-day trip on a ship, on an American army ship, and when they gave us breakfast on the American army ship there was jam on every table in the dining room, jam in any flavor you want. We didn't know what to do with it. We just kept eating it because it was such an exciting thing, such a good thing. I felt wonderful. So seeing the Statue of Liberty was overwhelming, it was just huge.

In the beginning, life was hard in America. But, we gradually started to get a good feeling about being here, a relaxed feeling about it. I was only with American kids now, and I just started to speak English. I don't know when and where exactly, it just happened. And when it did, I was the talk of the town, of Middle Village.

It was really not too bad. We had an apartment, and life was starting. We knew this was freedom.

PEARL K.
Poland

NITSAVIM

Choosing Life

I lived in Yugoslavia for five years after the war, and then I went to Israel. I married. I had children. I worked. I did not have the opportunity to go to school anymore, but it was a pioneering life and nice and free and very good to be young in Israel.

After the war, I did not want to speak about the Holocaust. I went passionately after the business of living and experiencing. I wanted to make up for all those lost years fast. I wanted to learn and to study and to know the music that was being played in the times when I wasn't around. As I was passionately going after this business of living, I felt such gratitude to those people that saved us. These were ordinary people that will never be in history books—that I unfortunately don't even remember their names and probably they are not alive anymore, and I probably wouldn't have even the emotional strength to find them if they were. But in an era when goodness was very rare, they cultivated it, and they showed that there was human decency and heroism, which was so rare in those times.

To be heroic is so unpredictable. They probably wouldn't have known themselves that they were going to behave the way they did. They simply reacted to our despair with compassion. They didn't think of themselves. They didn't care what happened to them. When you think that we were not family—we were not even friends—we were strangers that fell from somewhere into their laps and they never looked for excuses to say, Well we can't, I'm sorry, we have a young family, never. This is something that the post-Holocaust generation should know—that people have choices and the ones who saved us proved it.

ESTHER B.
Yugoslavia

Va-yelekh

Education

In the ghetto, all things like youth clubs and organizations were prohibited, but we had a cheder. We went right behind their backs, and we had schools. And we studied. I was studying. I was really advancing. I was learning Gemarah. Of course, there weren't any public schools or anything, but we used to go in the afternoon and study. We talk about this business of people not resisting and not running away and all this. But there was a resistance. We did resist.

We taught ourselves, people with talent performed, we sang and created poems. There was even entertainment. People went to the synagogue. We would take popular songs of the time and add different lyrics to them. Many of them were quite sad. Some of them were humorous, but the humor was gallows humor.

There was a song about Treblinka, which eventually everybody found out was a death camp. It went: Treblinka there—there is a place for every Jew—you can go in, but you can't come out—that is Treblinka.

All of this is totally prohibited, of course, under penalty of death, but they couldn't suppress that part of the spirit.

Leon L.
Poland

HA'AZINU

God

After the war, Lotte and I gradually consolidated our middle class aspirations into a family with two girls, our daughters, who were born in London in 1953 and 1957, our hope being that our daughters wouldn't be burdened particularly with our past. And so we are grateful to fate and grateful to the British for how things have turned out.

One asks oneself sometimes, Why did we have so much more luck than others? There is no answer to that. But it makes you wonder where is God. I don't want to offend anybody here now, but my religious notions are impossible to fit into any of the known religious groupings. I don't say I'm agnostic. I believe in God, but not in a man-made God, that's much too small a framework.

I have acquired a scientific-evolutionary outlook of the development of life on earth, and I feel there is some meaning behind our death which is all for some good reason kept mysterious to us. But I do pray. I do think of my parents and of all the other relatives and friends who perished, and I still cannot understand why, and I pray.

ERNEST K.
Austria-Hungary

דברים
Ve-zo't Ha-berakhah
Leadership

As we arrived in Brunlitz, we walked out of the boxcars and Oskar Schindler was standing there. We felt such a relief that here is the man who is going to protect us. We felt that maybe, maybe now we have a chance for survival. There was also a camp commander by the name of Leiport who was a beast, but Schindler kept him in line.

But the greatest thing that Schindler did is when the news came around February, beginning of February of 1945, that some boxcars were abandoned on a siding—four boxcars with Jews. Schindler went by himself and he found out that there really were Jewish people there. He came back to camp and organized two trucks with people, I among them, who would return to open the boxcars and get the people out. It was a very severe winter, and the doors of those boxcars were frozen, completely frozen, and we couldn't open them. So he sent back one truck to bring torches, and we lit up those doors with our torches, and we opened them. 80 percent of those people were dead by that time, and the 20 that were alive were walking skeletons. Whoever was alive, we put on a truck and we brought back to camp, and Schindler set up a hospital for them. He acquired cots, he bought black market food for them—milk and oatmeal and farina and all kind of things. He brought them back to life. They were Hungarian Jews and by the time the war was over, they were already functioning. They were still very thin, but they were functioning.

My speculation about why he did all this is that Schindler came as a black marketeer to Poland and his only aim was to make money, but he got to like those few Jews who were around him and he said, Why are they killing them? They're not such bad people. Besides, he was a bon vivant. He loved women, wine—he could drink, he could party. And, after two

81

or three years, it became like a sport for him—maybe he'll defy the Final Solution—maybe he'll beat the system, and he'll save those 1,100 Jews. Yeah, he was a man who loved life.

LEWIS F.
Poland

HOLIDAYS

חגים

Rosh Hashoneh was the selektzia—the selection about who was next to be killed. It was in the afternoon, three o'clock, four o'clock. We heard that Mengele was the head of these selektzia. And when he came he said, Look, that's it. Look, what's it? That was exactly erev Rosh Hashoneh. Everybody was sent back into the barracks. All of a sudden we hear cars coming, going, children crying, this and that, maybe for a half an hour. Now that night a rabbi came to blow the shofar in the backyard. From where he took the shofar I don't know up to today, but he did it.

Anyway, it must have been already late at night, all quiet. We had one guy I will never forget, he had a beautiful voice. That night he sang a little bit for the whole world, to daven. No one had a siddur, but we sang, crying and all that.

The next morning we went into the barracks across. Empty. In the wall, the walls were made out of wood, so in the walls were scratched in names, this name, this name, and this name. Then we first find out what's the story. That's what it was. They took them away. That was Rosh Hashoneh, and that's how it was until erev Yom Kippur.

By that time we were already so contemptible mentally, already so hardened, that it didn't bother us. That's the way it is, what could you do?

JONAS B.
Czechoslovakia

The Ten Days of Repentance עשרת ימי

In October 1944, we had the High Holy Days and we were allowed to take time off for services. Of course, they had to report to the Red Cross Commissions that came to inspect Terezin that they really did good things for the Jews. That Rosh Ha-shanah services were conducted by a Czech Cantor, Goldring, who came to the states and became a cantor in Indianapolis.

But Yom Kippur was reserved for my choir and me. The strange thing is every day trains were leaving and coming back, and the train whistles were haunting us without stopping, always to a point that we didn't hear it anymore, we ignored it. On the first day of Rosh Ha-shanah, there was no whistle. We noticed the absence of the whistle as something very strange. Of course, immediately, speculations. We knew that the Russian front was coming closer. The train whistle stopped. What a wonderful sign.

And sure enough the second day Rosh Ha-shanah, again services—not one train left the ghetto, no whistle. So for ten days we prayed and hoped. Comes Yom Kippur, the same thing. This had to be the end, it had to be. So we joyfully conducted our services in the highest spirits imaginable. It was a very hot day, I remember that, and we had to open the big windows of this huge hall. Outside, masses of people who couldn't get in were pushing themselves forward, ready to catch parts of the services the whole day. Fasting for us was very easy. Actually, we were experts at this, I would say, and our spirits were very, very high, just great.

At the end of this Yom Kippur service the shofar, the ram's horn, is blown. It is blown on Rosh Ha-shanah, the beginning of the year, to call people's attention, admonish them to seek—well, to search themselves, and offer prayers and ask forgiveness. So for ten days this is done. On this tenth day, this very long day, near the end of the concluding service, the neilah, at the end with the sun about to set, the shofar is blown once more. This shofar tone is called the big shofar tone. It's a tone that's to be held real long so it carries over into the days to follow.

As we reached that point, Cantor Levy from Berlin placed that shofar to his mouth and started to blow the shofar tone. This is something one waits for, this is the signal that gives you hope and all your prayers should be fulfilled at that point or from that point on. As he blew, he brought the most beautiful long-held tone. It was just unbelievable, until—and I remember this—it seemed to be off key. It was off key that very moment.

Whenever I think back, I think, did I make this up? No, I did not. At that moment, the tone that crept in there was the train whistle. At that important moment, at the height of our expectations, at the height of hope that our prayers would be fulfilled, the whistle starts. Again. We were stunned. We didn't know what to do, but we didn't have much time to think about it. The very next morning my brother and I were on the train to Auschwitz without delay.

KURT M.
Germany

KOL NIDRE

When people were in lager, in the concentration camp, they were so disappointed in the world, in culture, and in civilization. They were so disappointed. And a lot of them turned toward religion. When I used to say the Shema or some other prayers, they would join me, repeat after me, to have a little feeling. They also wanted to hear music that was recorded, so I sang the Ani Ma'amin for them. I was asked to sing it and I sang it quite often.

One night, we sat in a tunnel in Mauthausen. It was Kol Nidre night. I knew it was Kol Nidre because I kept the calendar. I got up and I said, Yidn—Jews, I'll sing for you Kol Nidre and I'll sing you Ani Ma'amin. Those who were there never forgot it.

The Ani Ma'amin is one of the 13 principles that Maimonides ordered Jews to say every day. The principle is: I believe, I believe with my full heart and full trust that the Messiah will come and redeem the world, and though he is tarrying, we certainly believe that eventually he is gonna come. This caught on. There were other prayers that could have given more religious satisfaction than the Ani Ma'amin, but this Ani Ma'amin sung with a certain melody caught on.

We sang that melody, which finally finishes in a march tempo, and we sang the Partisan Song: Never say that you are on your last leg, though leaden skies conceal the days of blue. The hour that we longed for will appear; our steps will beat like drums, we are still here! Somehow those songs broke through the walls and fences of the concentration camps. I don't know how, but they came.

ISAAC A.
Poland

YOM KIPPUR

It was Yom Kippur in Auschwitz. Somebody was keeping count and word got around, and at night in my particular block, women were singing the Kol Nidre. One of the girls, somebody who had probably a good voice, but more importantly, knew the melody and knew the words, and just—it was so quiet, when she sang—normally there were yells and screams and pushings and cryings and bickering among the inmates. We were miserable, we were terrible, we were hungry, we were frightened, and we were so lonely, so alone, so abandoned, we didn't know what was going on. And this night, you could hear a sigh, you could hear it when this woman sang the Kol Nidre.

The next morning we went out for Zählappell, roll call. They brought coffee, but nobody touched it. Came noon, and we stand in a single row and strangely, this time, the two barrels of what used to be just slop is being supervised by the SS. I don't know how it happened, but I was first in line, and he says, Komm, come. I go, and he lifts, and as I went a couple of steps, somehow instinctively I put both my hands behind my back including the tin cup, at which point the SS dips the ladle into the barrel of soup, lifts it, and lets it drip back, the soup, saying to me, Schön, nein? Nice, no?

But I remembered the night before, the chant, the Kol Nidre, and I say, Nein. He does it again, and I still keep my hands back. And then he takes the ladle with the soup and splashes it in my face and calls me Pig Jew. Now the soup drips down my face, and I have this urge to at least lick it because it's full of potatoes. I mean, he was showing it to me, that it was full of chunks of potatoes and meat, and here this thing is dripping down my face and I so want to lick it, but I didn't. I didn't. Came the next girl and she said,

Nein. Nobody took it. After I think the 10th or 15th girl, he kicked the barrel of soup over. Nobody touched it.

I really don't know what gave me the strength, I really don't know. I don't know whether I would have done it if the night before there wouldn't have been some sort of a Kol Nidre. I mean, that really evoked some very strong feelings of memories, of belonging somewhere, of being part of something, of having a legacy, a heritage.

That was the only moment that I think back while I was in Auschwitz that I did what I'm glad I did. It's not that I did anything bad or anything good, I was just a cog in the wheel, but I did something beyond what was expected of me.

Food was the most exciting, the most potent thing in Auschwitz, because food was life, food was power. But in that case, that Yom Kippur, it was not.

BARBARA F. T.
Romania

SHEMINI 'ATSERET

My father said we are going to look for some house, maybe we find some empty house, because the entire town was empty, ruined by the war. As we walked we saw that on many houses, destroyed houses, on many walls, there are inscriptions, different things, written by fingers which were dipped into blood. I remember one of those inscriptions: I, Moshe Yisroel, and my wife Feige, and my children, avenge us, avenge us—the murderers come.

Imagine these messages from the walls, telling us what happened in this place when the Romanians and the Germans exterminated all these Jews, and they called us for vengeance—that we should take revenge because of their deaths. My father stood and said kaddish. And Jews stood around with us, too. Hundreds.

Suddenly my father said to me like this—Yankele, we say kaddish, we say Yizkor on Shemini Atzeres but the day afterwards, we dance also with the Torah. And we went back to the place where we had this little Torah, from nowhere we got some table and we dance with the Torah in this scenery, on this background, in this house. It was a struggle to maintain human dignity, it was a struggle to maintain the relation with our past, it was a struggle to remain just human beings and I don't know where from my father took this strength.

Then we prayed around the Sefer Torah all the prayers of the holidays. On Simchas Torah, there is a Hatan Torah and I remember my father was reading from the Torah and he was also Hatan Torah. Years later, in my synagogue in Israel I got to be Hatan Torah from the same Sefer Torah. This Sefer Torah is actually in my synagogue in Israel, so I asked that I should read it in that Sefer Torah. I made the bracha and as I just start to read, I saw my father there, and I couldn't utter a single word. I started to cry and every word was just as difficult as to cross the Red Sea, but nobody understood why.

After, my wife and me, we gave a big Kiddush in the synagogue and as is usual, the Hatan Torah has to say some divrei Torah. Naturally, I prepared something. But by then I said to the entire congregation, My dear friends, this time I won't say any divrei Torah, but I'm going to tell you the story about the Torah. And, for the first time, I told this story to my congregation.

YAACOV R.
Romania

חגים

Simhat Torah

imchas Torah I liked. The dancing was always wonderful. But one Simchas Torah they decided to give the people who get called to the Torah funny hats. And so everybody had to wear a funny hat when they got called to the Torah.

They called Papa to the Torah, and they gave him a funny hat which was this kind of German Army hat with a pointed thing and in front of it they had a string. On the string was an egg that had been blown out, but filled with plaster of Paris, so it was pretty heavy on the string. And it was so that if you would shokel in the davening, it would bang you in the nose.

So they put this on Papa's head and called him to the Torah. And Papa goes, Barechu et Hashem Ham'voyrach, and hitting the people on the both sides. And I still remember that with—with joy.

ZALMAN S-S.
Poland

HANUKAH חנכה

After lighting the candles, we'd sing Ma'oz Tzur along with a wind-up tin music box that was in the base of the menorah. We kids got such a kick out of it because if you wound the spring all the way, it would play the song really fast and you had to sing along really fast, and as the spring in the music box expanded and corroded, Ma'oz Tzur got slower and it was easier to sing along.

Then we'd play dreidel for walnuts and apples. We didn't have any money, we were just kids. I would also play the Hanukah männleh, little man in our dialect, for my younger brother. I was about 13 or 14 years old. Many people in our small town did that so the kids wouldn't feel left out for Christmas.

I'd dress up in an old hat, a long coat, and a beard I made out of straw that the esrog for Sukkos came wrapped in, and I'd come and visit him and tell him to be a good boy and give him a present. When I came in later, my brother always wanted to know why I wasn't there when the Hanukah männleh came to visit him. Even when he got older and my parents told him the truth, he still didn't believe it was me.

JULIUS K.
Germany

94

My mother never could talk about the past. She was heartbroken—so I don't know too much about my past. But she didn't want to leave Poland because she was too old. In 1949, when I was 15, I tried to change religions, to become Catholic. I went to church every Sunday because I wanted be like everybody else. I had permission from the Bishop to become Catholic, and I was supposed to be baptized.

One day, one of my friends said, I saw you the other day with Jewish women. What were you doing with those Jewish women? Why do you even look at them or talk to them? And I said, These Jewish women are my sister and my mother. My friend—who was Polish and Catholic and who knew that I was converting—she said that I am Jewish, and that I will always be Jewish. Then I realized who I am. I said that whatever I will do, I will always be a Jew.

So then I start going once a year to synagogue with my mother. I only went once a year because there were not enough Jews in Krakow to have a service every Friday. And, at age 22, I decided I'm going to Israel. I want to be Jewish, I am going to Israel.

I ended up in Kibbutz Maagan Michael. I didn't speak Yiddish, so there they didn't think I'm Jewish—they thought I was Polish.

SOPHIA A.
Poland

אים PURIM

Purim was always a fun holiday for us. My mother made each of the kids a Haman man, which is like a gingerbread man only it's bigger. It was made out of yeast dough, about one foot tall and three inches thick, and my mother always made him a big belly. My mother put raisins for Haman's eyes, nose, and mouth, and walnuts down his belly for buttons.

My younger brother and I used to put raisins, you know, down there, or stole a little dough and made him a schmeckel and put it on, but my mother always caught us, laughed, and took it off.

After she baked Haman, we'd put a string around Haman's neck because he was hung, and then one of us would hold the string and the other would pull on Haman's body until his head came off. We'd spend the day eating him; sometimes it took two days, and we'd dunk him in malzkaffee, the coffee made from burned malt that my mother would make us. We weren't allowed real coffee. We got to eat Haman after we came home from the Megillah reading at shul, and I can still taste it all these years later.

JULIUS K.
Germany

We entered Germany in the spring of '45. And this was Aachen, the first German town that was captured by the enemy. I was in a replacement depot for reassignment, and I came in there, and I noticed it's getting close to Passover. So I came in and I says, Are there going to be any Passover services? So a fellow said, You have to get in touch with the Jewish chaplain. Well, how do I do that? He says, Tell me where you are and which tent you're in and when he comes back, I'll have him get in touch with you.

Later that night in comes this guy, he was a big, rough and tumble guy, and he says, I'm looking for Norman. I says, That's me and who are you? He says, I'm the chaplain, what can I do for you? I says, Well, I wanted to know if there's going to be any Passover services. It seems strange you know because we were cultural Jews and weren't very much into religion. But the holidays were very, very important in our home. He said, Boy, am I glad you're here. I could use you. You're going to be assigned to me and you're going to be my assistant, and I want you to find a place where we can have services. And just like that, boom, boom, boom, boom, here I am, strangely a chaplain's assistant.

So, I came to this building and it looked like a good building—it was standing, and it was big enough. It so happened it's the Aachen city hall. I walk in and I says, I want to see the mayor, and the mayor comes out and clicks his heels. I says, I'm looking for a place for a Passover seder. I'm Jewish, you know what that is? I says, I'm Jewish and we got to have a Passover service. And he turned every color of the rainbow. And, I says, this looks like a great building. Well, he swallowed 16 times and turned red, but he says

okay. I says, I'm gonna come back tomorrow and I want this place set up. I want there to be a place for about 200 people, you got enough room? He clicks his heels, yes, he'll have it.

People started straggling in—first of all came the rear echelon such as myself—and in every company there were some Jews I guess that came forward and they took their places. Then these guys from the frontline start traipsing in with their muddy boots and all their gear. We probably had maybe 150 or 175 people and as they came to the part in the service where it says, We were slaves unto the Pharaoh of Egypt, all of a sudden we turn around and see a whole bunch of young men—young men that looked old, they were scrawny and skinny and starved looking and they were wearing their striped uniforms. They were slaves to Hitler, of course—survivors. Somehow—because remember we still hadn't gotten to the concentration camps, but somehow they got free and they came and everybody was crying.

We were all crying, all for different reasons. I don't know if we ever finished the service—but we were crying. To see so many grown men cry—very strange. But there was just so much going through us.

It was probably the most emotional experience of my life—to think that all these people, somehow, by some miracle got together on Passover. I'll never forget it.

NORMAN M.
United States

LAST DAYS OF PESAH

Since I can remember, my mother always made göttespeise and put it on top of krimsel for dessert at the seders and for the last days of Pesah. Göttespeise is German for food of the gods, and it truly is. It's a wine cream made by cooking egg yolks, sugar, wine, lemon and potato starch. When it's cool, stiffened egg whites are folded in. We'd beat the egg whites by hand—we never owned a beater. The göttespeise is put over krimsel, which are matzah pancakes made with matzah, and of course with lots of eggs and sugar, fruit and wine, and then fried up.

Having krimsel with göttespeise was truly like being in heaven for a little girl. Because of the whipped egg whites, it only lasted a few hours, so we'd eat it all up right away. I looked forward to it all year.

When we came to America, we still made it. I taught my daughter how to make it, and it's very special to see her make it for the seder. Once, my son's friend, who is a chef, asked me for lessons on how to make krimsel. It was in January, and I showed him how, but it didn't taste the same. It wasn't Pesah.

MARGOT S. K.
Germany

At the end of the war, in Belgrade, there was a parade. We partisans marched in the parade. People would come up, put cigarettes in our pocket, money in our pocket, because we marched in the Jewish contingent. Wherever we marched we heard, Long live the liberated Jews. I could easily break down now when I think of it, particularly because the contrast was so dreadful when I finally reached the Hungarian border. There we saw many atrocities.

Once I was with the partisans and I was put into a propaganda unit. We were taken to a place where 400, if not more, of my friends from the neighboring camp I had been in were shot and thrown into a mass grave. I think that many more were shot there, massacred by the SS, but I only know about these 400.

I think it was near Majdanek, but I'm not sure about the location now. I've got a very hazy concept about the time frame, because basically I know that we are looking at a very short time period, but so much happened and it was so eventful that when I look back on it, it seems to be years and years and years. But, when I try to fit the events I remember into a rational time scale and chronology, I just can't manage. You know, it's sort of like when you dig a hole, the earth never fits back.

STEPHEN G.
Romania

YOM HA-'ATSM'AUT

My first questioning—it wasn't real questioning, it was puzzlement—was how this could happen. And I remember my mother put it extremely well to a Rabbi Liss who had been influential in the small yeshiva of Shanghai. She asked him one day in my presence: How could God have permitted the most learned, the most Jewish part of the community, to be destroyed? And he used the Yiddish phrase, If you hit someone you hit them in the face. I never understood the logic of that. It was a continual puzzle to me. And I studied and I prayed, but I couldn't figure out how this could happen if there were a merciful—and I kept saying, He is a merciful God, He is a just God, then how could this happen? It was very difficult.

I think the major thing which saved me from being more distraught than I was, was the fact that my bar mitzvah was approaching and my bar mitzvah would be a major event. My teachers in the yeshiva wanted me to read a whole section of the Torah. Of course, that was understood, and the Haftarah. Then I was being tutored to hold a speech and I worked on that. Then something called a pshetl. A pshetl is a commentary on the Talmud. So fortunately for me a lot of my time was being taken up by these preparations. And throughout this, there was the feeling about how could this God that I was praying to have permitted this to happen.

The day of my bar mitzvah arrived. It was going to be held in my father's synagogue—not the yeshiva—and then a truly magical thing happened. As I went to shul that morning and the services began, an American, a captain in the American army, came in. It ended up that this captain was actually a rabbi. What was so hard about this was that at the same time I was hearing about the Holocaust, I was seeing an American officer who was obviously an honored person who wore a Mogen Dovid on his lapel. It was very puzzling for a God to permit this at the same time. I had enormous difficulty reconciling this in my mind.

He had just been rotated through Shanghai on Friday and found the synagogue and he showed up at services. Obviously, he was the most honored guest immediately. His name was Gordon. He gave a very brief and extremely moving speech, saying he didn't know if he would find any Jews in Shanghai when he came—he certainly didn't know whether he'd find a service, and when he found a service, he said he was absolutely amazed to find a bar mitzvah. And then he said something which broke me up then as it does now—he said the words, Am Yisroel Chai—Am Yisroel Chai means the Jewish people will live, now and forever.

There wasn't anybody in that synagogue who wasn't crying at that because the majority of our relatives hadn't made it and suddenly there was a great occasion, a happy occasion. There was also the feeling of hope that there was a country where Jews were not persecuted. Even the rabbi would be an officer, an honored officer, and at the same time you had this other thing going on, so it was very complicated, encouraging, wonderful and sad. The contrasts were incredible and that was the most memorable for me—what I did was less important than what Gordon said, Am Yisroel Chai, that the Jewish people is alive forever.

SIGMUND T.
Germany

I was in a familienlager, a family camp, and we had quite an organized thing for children. It wasn't food, it wasn't fun, but what we did have was education. The classes were not secret, the Nazis knew about them, but it wasn't like a classroom. We would kind of concentrate in one part of the sleeping area. They divided us by age groups and people would teach us. I remember that there were some very good teachers, and that I learned about poetry, and I learned about music, and somebody even told us how movies are made. We learned Beethoven's Ninth and were singing that in German.

They tried to keep us busy and one man, Freddy Hirsch, was coming and organizing the whole thing. I remember one time that he called all the children outside and he was teaching us about self-hypnosis. He was lecturing us, that if we suffer from anything—if something hurts—if we are hungry—we can help ourselves by telling ourselves it isn't so. If we have pain—we say the pain is going away—it's going away—it's going and it's gone—you know this has been working for me all my life. If I was hungry, I was telling myself I wasn't—it's going away—it's going away—it's gone. I can still do it today.

I don't know what saved my life—I think that stupidity saved my life—the fact that I didn't understand what was going on. I didn't understand the unfairness of it—I was just concerned with survival, but those lessons helped me to survive.

CHAVA B-A.
Czechoslovakia

תשעה באב

TISHA' BE-'AV

They masterminded everything so precisely. On Tisha'
Be-'Av, I remember it very well. On Tisha' Be-'Av, it
was I don't know what date, but we didn't go to
work. Of course, most of us fasted. I wouldn't say everybody
fasted, but most of us.

So they decided to make a concert. So the local talent—
there was some girl that was singing—but one was doing a
pantomime, how they come to go to the crematoria—and I'll
never forget it. You know, I don't know the name, nothing,
all the Germans were there—they were clapping, they were
enjoying themselves. I don't know who she was and what she
was, but she was, you know, with a suitcase and going, you
know, like dressed funny and they were just hilarious
enjoying themselves. And there were a few skits like whoever
could do what and even that time they gave us a better lunch
than usually—that was the only decent lunch—on Tisha'
Be-'Av, just because they knew that we cannot eat.

And then I read in one article a lady from Romania
wrote—she was in the big camp, she was a doctor, a
gynecologist—that they had a concert in the big camp—a
musical. Just music and everybody had to go and listen.

SHIRLEY G.
Czechoslovakia

FRIDAY NIGHT I

חיים

E ven in hiding, we remained aware of the Jewish
calendar. First of all, we were always lighting—my
mother was always lighting Shabbos candles. They
would be hollowed out of half a potato with a little bit of oil
and a piece of thread or cotton.

My mother would light these candles every Friday and Mr.
Bermaszewich when he was in a bad mood would say, They
are going to find us all because of those candles. Somebody
will see them and they'll figure out that there are Jews here,
and they'll find us, and they'll drag us out, and they'll kill all
of us. But he also said that if we will survive, it's because of
my mother's faith, because she's behaving like a holy person.

Now, a few weeks before Passover, she told Mrs.
Bermaszewich that she would like to make Passover. No, she
told her. But mother said, I can make such a good borscht as
you never ate before. For that, I need beets and I need water
and a glass jar. She made borscht. A holy person.

NECHAMA A.
Poland

FRIDAY NIGHT II

We began to feel more distinctly how the ghetto was being emptied. We realized our turn would be coming soon. All the lovely things we did in the lovely Terezin. It was done all under pressure, to retain our own dignity. That's what they wanted to take away from us, our dignity. That we had to fight for. And in that respect, we succeeded.

Not that we all of a sudden felt superior, but we insisted on being ourselves, no matter how hard it was, how hard the circumstances were. Each block elder had to supply the Jewish administration every morning with a number of people they selected for the next deportation. A miserable job, but it had to be done—there was no way out, we just accepted it, because we were completely powerless in this situation.

But we continued conducting our services. The services were held during the summer in the open, in the courtyard. Masses of people came there every Friday night, and we sang with a choir and the real music they remembered from their homes, whether Berlin or Vienna. Basically the same melodies so they could join, and they're praying. If anybody had reason to pray, it was us.

In the wintertime, because we couldn't do it outside, we went to the attic, a very, very small area, with all these beams going every which way. We squeezed in there and I haven't prayed like this in the United States, with that intensity, not one single time. Not that I want to wish for having to pray this way. And so we did this, and this was very successful. It gave people hope and faith in the midst of all things that were happening.

KURT M.
Germany

שבת SHABBAT

Saturday afternoon, my grandmother and I danced the waltzes. She loved movies that she couldn't go because of my grandfather, he was quite religious. But what she did do for me was in the winter time and all through my childhood, on Saturday afternoon I got in bed with her, and she read to me the Torah, the Haftorah, in Yiddish, and I loved it.

When I memorized it, I went out in the street and I told the kids for money. I told them the story of Abraham and of Joseph. Joseph and Benjamin were my favorites.

CATHERINE L.
Czechoslovakia

Shabbat, I used to go to my grand grandfather, Reb Chaim Eisenthal, who was a big erudite, a talmid, a disciple of the Berischaner Rav, which was a very famous rabbi at that time in Poland. He used to test me, to examine me, to see if I remember what I studied in the cheder.

He had this little shop next to his house, and at the end, he went to his shop and took out a red candy that he gave me. You don't know what a taste has such a candy. That was the recompense when I knew well. Even if I didn't know so well, also I got a candy.

Also, especially in the summertime for the seudah sh'lishit, we all went to the grandfather. At that time we liked very much strawberries, but not that you buy here from the grocery stores, but strawberries that have been picked in the woods, little strawberries. This with sour cream, that was a real pleasure. And for me, he added a lot of sugar on that.

YAACOV R.
Romania

TESTIMONIES

CLAL gratefully acknowledges USC Shoah Foundation Institute for Visual History and Education, University of Southern California, for allowing us to use the following testimonies:

Interviewee	Date of Interview	Place of Interview
A., Ada	3 July 1996	Whitestone, New York
A., Cila	16 February 1998	Los Angeles, California
A., Curt	12 October 1997	Lacey, Washington
A., David	4 November 1997	Brooklyn, New York
A., Gabor	10 March 1997	St. Laurent, Quebec, Canada
A., Harry	20 January 1995	Brooklyn, New York
A., Herbert	5 July 1996	Los Angeles, California
A., Irene	2 February 1997	Falls Church, Virginia
A., Isaac	9 February 1997	West Hartford, Connecticut
A., Mark	5 January 1997	New Haven, Connecticut
A., Nechama	10 December 1997	Brooklyn, New York
A., Ruth	10 July 1996	Sharon, Massachusetts
A., Sophia	10 September 1996	West Hartford, Connecticut
B., Charlotte	19 June 1997	London, Greater London, England
B-A., Chava	10 April 1997	Jamaica, New York
B., Esther	3 February 1995	Don Mills, Ontario, Canada
B., Eta	15 February 1996	Brooklyn, New York
B., Eugene	27 April 1997	Pool-In-Wharfdale, West Yorkshire, England
B., Jerzy	11 April 1995	Wollstonecraft, Sydney, NSW, Australia
B., Jonas	11 July 1996	Brooklyn, New York

B., Leo	8 June 1997	Cerritos, California
B., Mila	25 July 1995	Passaic, New Jersey
B., Rebecca	14 March 1995	North York, Ontario, Canada
B., Ruth	13 June 1996	Mill Hill, London, Greater London, England
B., Shony	22 March 1995	Los Angeles, California
C., Peter	5 December 1996	Natick, Massachusetts
C., Robert	12 September 1994	Beverly Hills, California
D., Reidar	3 October 1999	Northfield, Minnesota
D., Renee	14 May 1997	Daly City, California
E., Jack	21 July 1997	Redlands, California
F., Akiva	7 August 1996	Willowdale, Ontario, Canada
F. T., Barbara	27 March 1995	New York, New York
F., Joseph	4 February 1997	El Cerrito, California
F., Lewis	27 March 1995	Boca Raton, Florida
F., Mordechi	17 November 1996	Baltimore, Maryland
F., Rena	23 October 1996	Framingham, Massachusetts
F., Tova	22 November 1998	Highland Park, New Jersey
G., Bella	3 January 1997	Kew Gardens, New York
G., George	24 September 1996	Hallendale, Florida
G., Gustav	30 January 1997	Silver Spring, Maryland
G., Regina	5 August 1996	San Diego, California
G., Shirley	23 June 1998	Millville, New Jersey
G., Stephen	24 April 1996	Elizabeth Bay, Sydney, NSW, Australia
K., Adam	8 December 1996	Toorak, Victoria, Australia
K., Ernest	2 July 1996	London, Greater London, England
K., Moses	20 June 1996	Glendale, New York
K., Pearl	22 June 1997	Bayside, New York
L., Catherine	27 May 1997	Chevy Chase, Maryland
L., Estelle	23 October 1996	Kensington, Maryland

L., Leon	16 November 1995	Fullerton, California
M., Akiva Yossef	29 August 1996	Toronto, Ontario, Canada
M., Kurt	24 June 1997	Portland, Maine
M., Norman	17 June 1998	Bloomfield Hills, Michigan
P., Francis Joseph	14 September 1997	Melbourne, Victoria, Australia
P., Paul	23 October 1995	Boston, Massachusetts
R., Betty	23 December 1996	Lakeworth, Florida
R., Charles	30 October 1997	Dresher, Pennsylvania
R., Clara	15 July 1997	Toronto, Ontario, Canada
R., Edward	16 June 1997	Caulfield North, Melbourne, Victoria, Australia
R., Sophie	19 August 1996	Brooklyn, New York
R., Yaacov	24 July 1996	Brooklyn, New York
S., Lester	25 November 1997	Cedarhurst, New York
S-S., Zalman	23 March 1998	Boulder, Colorado
T., Sigmund	30 October 1997	Teaneck, New Jersey
V., Laura	11 March 1997	Seattle, Washington

AFTERWORD

A LOVE of the Jewish people

A DESIRE to perpetuate the memory of the Holocaust

A VISION of people celebrating life while remembering loss

AN UNDERSTANDING that Torah is continually being written

These values are what brought Sherman Jacobson to CLAL. He wanted to publish a book of stories from the Holocaust that could be read each Shabbat and on holidays so that as we celebrate life today, we would remember yesterday.

CLAL, which helped Americans begin to face and address the Holocaust in the 1970s, was instrumental in the creation of the United States Holocaust Memorial Council and Museum. Now, thirty years later, thanks to the vision, determination and tireless energy of Sherman Jacobson, and the generous support of a large group of caring and concerned donors, we at CLAL are proud to bring this important new work to the American Jewish community.

We are deeply appreciative of the generosity, support and assistance of the USC Shoah Foundation Institute for Visual History and Education, University of Southern California, which made its vast archives of interviews with survivors of the Holocaust available to us for this special project.

We want to thank Rabbi Richard Eisenberg for introducing CLAL to Mr. Jacobson and Rabbi Irwin Kula for introducing us to the Jewish Publication Society. We also wish to acknowledge and thank CLAL staff members Judy Epstein, Aliza J. Kaplan and Janet R. Kirchheimer for their tireless work and dedication in producing the book.

Donna M. Rosenthal
Executive Vice Chairman
CLAL

Brad Hirschfield
President
CLAL

We gratefully acknowledge the support of the following people
who made this book possible:

Lucille Alderman
New Haven, CT

Ruthann and David Beckerman
Guilford, CT

Eileen and Andrew Eder
Guilford, CT

Ruth and Sherman Jacobson
Orange, CT

Doris and Simon Konover
West Hartford, CT

Gail and Richard Kwal
Boca Raton, FL

Helaine and Marvin Lender
Woodbridge, CT

Evelyn and Bruce Rabison
Lantana, FL

Dr. Caren Jacobson Roberts and Dr. Blair Roberts
North Andover, MA

Lynne Jacobson Schpero and Dr. Mark Schpero
New Haven, CT

Susan Jacobson Schwartz
Farmington, CT

Arlene and Arnold Shanbrom
New Haven, CT

Harriet and Seymour Shapiro
New Haven, CT

Phyllis and Ronald Shaw
Woodbridge, CT

Sigmund Strochlitz
New London, CT

Janice and Stanley Sussman
Milford, CT

Shirley and Morris Trachten
New Haven, Ct

Lillian and Leon Weinberg
Hamden, CT

Sylvia and Michael Zamkov
New Haven, CT

INDEX